How to Use this Bool

Use these math tests as pre-assessments or post- assessments of students' skills. These math tests can be administered as a whole group, small group or when working individually with students.

Teacher Tips

➢ Review instructions for students to ensure understanding of the questions.

➢ Encourage students to complete the answers they know how to do first.

➢ Provide math manipulatives and other concrete materials for students to use during testing.

Math Rubric

Use the math rubric to help students to take responsibility for their learning and to assess their own math work.

Math Tests Record

This black line master will assist in keeping records.

Anecdotal Observations

Anecdotal observations give good insight to a student's understanding and application of math concepts.

Table of Contents

Number Sense and Numeration Tests

Name _____   **Addition Facts 0-12   #1**

5	1	2	7	6	8	4
+ 8	+ 6	+ 8	+ 5	+ 3	+ 0	+ 6

3	10	7	3	2	8	4
+ 4	+ 3	+ 9	+ 2	+10	+ 3	+ 2

9	1	5	4	5	9	Number Correct:
+ 5	+ 2	+ 6	+ 1	+ 10	+ 3	___ 20

Name _____   **Addition Facts 0-12   #2**

6	1	2	7	6	4	5
+ 3	+ 2	+ 0	+ 5	+ 7	+ 6	+ 2

3	10	7	4	2	8	4
+ 7	+ 4	+ 5	+ 4	+10	+ 2	+ 9

6	1	3	4	5	9	Number Correct:
+ 1	+ 3	+ 5	+ 7	+ 6	+ 0	___ 20

2 + 4	5 + 2	1 + 5	2 + 9	6 + 0	1 + 8	4 + 6
3 + 7	3 + 3	10 + 2	6 +4	2 +10	8 + 3	4 + 0
5 + 5	7 + 2	1 + 8	4 + 5	7 + 4	0 + 9	

Number
Correct:

_____
20

3 + 5	9 + 2	1 + 0	7 + 3	3 + 8	6 + 6	8 + 2
3 + 4	2 + 4	1 + 5	4 + 7	0 +10	2 + 2	3 + 9
4 + 2	6 + 3	5 + 7	6 + 5	1 + 6	3 + 0	

Number
Correct:

_____
20

Name _____

2 + 9	5 + 8	6 + 5	4 + 10	8 + 8	10 + 8	7 + 6
6 + 6	9 + 5	8 + 7	6 + 4	3 +10	8 + 9	9 + 9
5 +10	10 + 9	9 + 4	8 + 6	7 + 7	10 + 1	

Number Correct:

_____
20

Name _____

8 + 5	9 + 6	1 + 10	7 + 6	3 + 7	6 + 6	8 + 4
3 + 8	2 + 9	7 + 5	3 + 10	10 + 10	10 + 4	3 + 9
4 + 7	6 + 8	10 + 5	6 + 6	7 + 9	7 + 10	

Number Correct:

_____
20

Name _____

8	9	5	7	6	6	4
+ 6	+ 5	+ 5	+ 7	+ 7	+ 5	+ 9

7	10	8	6	10	8	3
+ 4	+ 6	+ 9	+6	+10	+ 3	+ 9

4	10	9	8	2	10	
+ 6	+ 0	+ 1	+ 8	+ 9	+ 7	

Number Correct:

——

20

Name _____

9	9	8	3	7	6	9
+ 9	+ 8	+ 7	+ 10	+ 9	+ 9	+ 8

4	7	10	3	4	10	9
+ 10	+ 5	+ 9	+ 7	+ 8	+ 3	+ 2

10	8	5	1	9	0	
+ 5	+ 2	+ 8	+ 10	+ 4	+ 10	

Number Correct:

——

20

82	92	50	78	65	41	43
+ 64	+ 56	+ 52	+ 11	+ 34	+15	+ 30

79	10	33	14	30	82	31
+ 10	+ 63	+ 42	+62	+17	+ 34	+ 90

15	22	45	80	42	10
+ 63	+ 75	+ 54	+ 16	+ 53	+77

Number Correct:

_____

20

Name _____   **Double Digit Addition #2**

12	80	48	73	37	66	18
+ 64	+ 17	+ 61	+ 10	+ 52	+ 93	+ 81

49	85	22	33	54	70	62
+ 10	+ 52	+ 66	+ 70	+ 84	+23	+ 14

20	49	35	10	24	30
+ 55	+ 30	+ 84	+ 10	+ 45	+ 10

Number Correct:

_____

20

Name _____ **Double Digit Addition: Regrouping #1**

79	31	18	27	16	48	63
+ 12	+ 59	+ 68	+ 53	+ 46	+35	+27

19	34	76	15	23	22	39
+61	+ 47	+ 17	+ 75	+ 48	+ 38	+ 13

89	45	45	28	35	14	
+ 14	+ 56	+ 47	+ 76	+ 55	+ 77	

Number Correct:

____

20

Name _____ **Double Digit Addition: Regrouping #2**

12	28	48	73	37	39	18
+ 69	+ 27	+ 36	+ 19	+ 54	+ 13	+ 28

49	35	25	33	29	37	66
+ 17	+ 56	+ 66	+ 38	+ 84	+23	+ 14

25	49	15	19	27	17	
+ 55	+ 45	+ 88	+ 19	+ 45	+ 27	

Number Correct:

____

20

10	6	11	7	6	8	10
- 8	-6	- 8	- 5	- 3	- 0	- 6

4	10	12	3	2	8	7
- 4	- 3	- 9	- 2	- 1	- 3	- 2

7	5	8	4	5	9
- 5	- 2	- 6	- 1	- 0	- 3

Number Correct:

_____
20

9	6	2	3	6	7	5
-5	- 3	- 2	- 0	- 2	- 6	- 4

8	10	12	6	12	8	11
- 4	-7	- 4	- 5	-10	- 2	- 9

7	6	9	8	11	9
- 4	- 1	- 3	- 5	- 6	- 0

Number Correct:

_____
20

10	11	7	8	6	8	10
- 9	- 7	- 6	- 5	- 3	- 4	- 2

4	12	10	3	2	8	7
- 1	- 8	- 4	- 2	- 1	- 5	- 6

7	8	5	6	8	9
- 4	- 4	- 1	- 1	- 0	- 7

Number Correct:

_____

20

6	9	7	4	5	9	5
- 3	- 7	- 3	- 2	- 0	- 6	- 4

10	8	12	12	6	3	11
- 8	- 4	-10	- 9	- 5	- 1	- 9

6	12	11	9	8	9
- 5	- 6	- 2	- 4	- 3	- 0

Number Correct:

_____

20

12	11	14	16	13	17	10
- 8	- 6	- 8	- 7	- 9	- 7	- 6

12	13	12	18	15	11	16
- 4	- 3	- 7	- 9	- 5	- 3	- 9

18	20	15	10	11	14
- 8	-10	- 6	- 9	- 9	- 7

Number Correct:

_____

20

11	14	12	16	13	17	10
- 8	- 6	- 5	- 6	- 4	- 10	- 2

13	12	12	18	15	11	17
- 6	- 3	- 2	- 7	- 7	- 4	- 9

20	15	18	10	11	14
- 9	- 7	- 9	- 1	- 2	- 4

Number Correct:

_____

20

14	13	12	11	16	18	10
- 8	- 5	- 3	- 1	- 6	- 9	- 7

12	15	12	13	17	11	16
- 7	- 5	- 6	- 5	- 9	-10	- 8

15	11	19	20	10	14	Number Correct:
- 9	- 6	- 9	-10	- 3	- 7	_____ 20

14	16	11	12	13	17	10
- 5	- 9	- 4	- 7	- 6	- 7	- 5

12	19	14	12	15	11	17
- 1	- 5	- 5	- 5	- 7	- 8	-8

15	10	20	18	11	14	Number Correct:
- 9	- 0	- 5	- 8	- 4	- 4	_____ 20

Name _____   **Double Digit Subtraction #1**

34 − 21	72 − 50	53 − 23	49 − 27	38 − 18	25 − 24	37 − 26
56 − 34	91 − 10	38 − 26	89 − 41	37 − 12	76 − 34	65 − 25
95 − 32	72 − 10	64 − 23	59 − 28	64 − 51	33 − 21	

Number Correct:

_____

20

Name _____   **Double Digit Subtraction #2**

93 − 73	64 − 31	82 − 60	75 − 40	48 − 32	35 − 24	27 − 15
37 − 20	39 − 24	68 − 52	84 − 42	32 − 12	97 − 34	65 − 23
48 − 36	92 − 30	59 − 10	89 − 58	34 − 31	71 − 60	

Number Correct:

_____

20

Name _____

Double Digit Subtraction with Regrouping #1

97	71	61	49	75	66	81
- 29	- 69	- 14	- 27	- 26	- 59	- 25

84	91	31	82	37	66	90
- 77	- 28	- 16	- 45	- 18	- 39	- 29

74	72	51	48	60	53	Number Correct:
- 17	- 18	- 23	- 29	- 41	- 28	___
						20

Name _____

Double Digit Subtraction with Regrouping #2

64	82	70	42	97	34	25
- 38	- 69	- 46	- 38	- 73	- 25	- 17

44	62	82	50	30	94	73
- 39	- 55	- 43	- 31	- 26	- 37	- 25

92	70	88	51	41	70	Number Correct:
- 30	- 49	- 59	- 34	- 36	- 13	___
						20

```
  419      497      827       146      732      336      543
+ 176    + 286    + 155     + 590    + 149    + 527    + 257


  708      837      693       748      406      586      717
+ 123    + 109    + 176     + 188    + 259    + 122    + 244


  365      260      684       578      791      584
+ 472    + 295    + 285     + 330    + 165    + 230
```

| Number Correct: |
| _____ |
| 20 |

```
  290      160      362       628      648      724      788
+ 130    + 594    + 353     + 136    + 168    + 419    + 123


  192      507      431       484      642      536      158
+ 589    + 308    + 388     + 243    + 199    + 156    + 619


  407      665      385       783      453      238
+ 399    + 119    + 140     + 142    + 350    + 257
```

| Number Correct: |
| _____ |
| 20 |

```
  662      493      821      846      739      936      446
 -476     - 286    - 155    - 590    - 249    - 527    - 257
```

```
  708      832      693      518      406      516      717
 - 123    -309     -376     -188     - 252    -122     - 243
```

```
  765      260      684      570      791      534
 - 472    - 135    - 285    - 318    - 165    - 280
```

Number Correct:
_____
20

```
  290      764      862      628      848      724      680
 -139     - 592    - 353    -136     - 163    - 419    - 123
```

```
  692      547      431      484      642      571      958
 - 379    - 309    - 308    - 246    - 129    - 256    - 629
```

```
  607      665      380      783      450      938
 - 394    - 129    - 145    - 148    - 153    - 257
```

Number Correct:
_____
20

$4.74	$5.83	$9.62	$2.60	$4.63	$1.82	$7.83
+ $2.62	- $1.25	- $7.32	+ $2.79	- $3.14	+ $4.41	- $5.26

$8.25	$9.42	$5.60	$4.50	$7.46	$3.00	$9.42
- $2.37	- $4.12	+ $3.75	- $0.50	- $5.12	+ $0.75	- $4.13

$5.74	$1.80	$9.66	$1.97	$4.81	$2.18	
+ $3.62	+ $5.25	- $3.18	+ $2.06	- $3.22	+ $1.43	

Number Correct:

_____

20

$3.74	$9.02	$4.69	$7.81	$7.23	$4.82	$2.74
+ $5.19	- $3.32	+ $4.79	- $4.55	- $5.19	+ $3.18	+ $2.62

$8.25	$1.25	$5.50	$9.42	$7.46	$7.00	$8.28
- $1.58	+ $3.80	- $0.50	- $3.80	- $5.12	+ $0.75	- $1.33

$2.84	$9.14	$2.17	$2.80	$4.33	$6.18	
+ $6.62	- $3.08	+ $4.06	+ $5.30	- $1.99	+ $3.48	

Number Correct:

_____

20

Name _____   **Multiplication Facts 1-5   #1**

2	4	5	8	6	10	7
X 5	X 2	X 4	X 1	X 3	x 2	X 3

6	6	9	3	3	8	8
X 4	X 3	X 5	X 2	X 4	X 1	X 5

1	8	10	7	7	10
X 4	X 1	X 3	X 5	X 2	X 1

Number Correct:

_____

20

Name _____   **Multiplication Facts 1-5   #2**

7	6	3	5	5	8	4
X 4	X 1	X 5	X 2	X 3	x 2	X 3

10	9	8	7	1	2	3
X 5	X 2	X 4	X 3	X 4	X 1	X 4

3	6	4	5	8	3
X 3	X 5	X 4	X 1	X 2	X 1

Number Correct:

_____

20

8	2	4	5	6	10	1
X 7	X 6	X 10	X 8	X 9	x 10	X 6

3	4	6	9	2	8	8
X 10	X 7	X 8	X 9	X 8	X 6	X 9

7	1	8	10	5	10
X 6	X 9	X 8	X 7	X 6	X 9

Number Correct:

_____

20

2	4	5	8	9	5	3
X 7	X 6	X 9	X 3	X 10	x 6	X 7

9	3	3	8	1	4	5
X 8	X 7	X 9	X10	X 10	X 9	X 8

6	3	4	7	9	5
X 10	X 6	X 8	X 8	X 6	X 7

Number Correct:

_____

20

Name _____

$10 \div 5 =$ $6 \div 2 =$ $15 \div 5 =$ $18 \div 2 =$ $2 \div 1 =$ $24 \div 4 =$ $25 \div 5 =$

$20 \div 4 =$ $4 \div 1 =$ $9 \div 3 =$ $18 \div 3 =$ $20 \div 2 =$ $28 \div 4 =$ $4 \div 4 =$

$21 \div 3 =$ $10 \div 2 =$ $12 \div 2 =$ $36 \div 4 =$ $27 \div 3 =$ $30 \div 6 =$

Number Correct:
_____
20

Name _____

Division Facts 1-5   #2

$8 \div 2 =$ $5 \div 5 =$ $16 \div 2 =$ $12 \div 4 =$ $45 \div 5 =$ $1 \div 1 =$ $30 \div 5 =$

$18 \div 3 =$ $32 \div 4 =$ $7 \div 1 =$ $28 \div 7 =$ $30 \div 3 =$ $14 \div 2 =$ $3 \div 1 =$

$16 \div 4 =$ $12 \div 3 =$ $4 \div 2 =$ $35 \div 5 =$ $40 \div 4 =$ $21 \div 7 =$

Number Correct:
_____
20

80 ÷ 10 =   35 ÷ 7 =   18 ÷ 9 =   12 ÷ 6 =   45 ÷ 5 =   10 ÷ 10 =   30 ÷ 10=

18 ÷ 9 =   32 ÷ 8 =   24 ÷ 6=   32 ÷ 4 =   35 ÷ 5=   48 ÷ 6 =   49 ÷ 7=

63 ÷ 9 =   14 ÷ 7 =   64 ÷ 8=   30 ÷ 6 =   40 ÷ 10 =   45 ÷ 9 =

Number Correct:

_____

20

90 ÷ 10 =   20 ÷ 10 =   6 ÷ 6 =   42 ÷ 7 =   27 ÷ 9 =   40 ÷ 5 =   30 ÷ 3=

81 ÷ 9 =   72 ÷ 8 =   48 ÷ 8 =   56 ÷ 8 =   36 ÷ 6=   35 ÷ 7=   70 ÷ 7=

72 ÷ 9 =   36 ÷ 9 =   54 ÷ 6 =   28 ÷ 7 =   80 ÷ 8=   40 ÷ 4 =

Number Correct:

_____

20

4 ÷ 4 =	10 ÷ 10 =	35 ÷ 7 =	45 ÷ 5 =	72 ÷ 8 =	16 ÷ 2 =	10 ÷ 5 =
16 ÷ 4 =	9 ÷ 3 =	32 ÷ 8 =	21 ÷ 3 =	42 ÷ 7 =	48 ÷ 6 =	49 ÷ 7 =
40 ÷ 8 =	90 ÷ 9 =	14 ÷ 2 =	30 ÷ 6 =	40 ÷ 10 =	72 ÷ 9 =	

Number Correct:

_____

20

20 ÷ 5 =	50 ÷ 10 =	6 ÷ 6 =	27 ÷ 3 =	27 ÷ 9 =	40 ÷ 5 =	3 ÷ 1 =
81 ÷ 9 =	8 ÷ 4 =	40 ÷ 4 =	56 ÷ 8 =	32 ÷ 4 =	48 ÷ 7 =	20 ÷ 2 =
72 ÷ 9 =	6 ÷ 2 =	54 ÷ 6 =	28 ÷ 7 =	8 ÷ 8 =	40 ÷ 10 =	

Number Correct:

_____

20

Addition and Subtraction Facts to 20

A. Add or subtract the following.

1.　3 　+ 9	2.　6 　- 2	3.　4 　+ 4	4.　18 　- 9	5.　5 　+ 6
6.　13 　- 7	7.　2 　+ 2	8.　11 　- 3	9.　2 　+ 8	10.　15 　- 6

B. Solve the following problems.

Show your work.

1. There were 12 ants on a log. 6 ants crawled away. How many ants were left on the log? There were _____ ants left.	
2. There were 7 girls and 6 boys playing hockey. How many children were playing hockey altogether? _____ children were playing.	

C. Circle the missing sign.

4 ◯ 8 = 12	+　　—　　=

Math Test:
Double Digit Addition and Subtraction

A. Add or subtract the following.

1. 67 - 25	2. 37 +52	3. 82 - 41	4. 59 - 37	5. 35 + 52
6. 25 - 14	7. 16 +82	8. 28 + 71	9. 57 +20	10. 48 - 17

B. Solve the following problems.

Show your work.

1. There were 67 jelly beans in a jar. 33 of the jelly beans were eaten. How many jelly beans were left in the jar? There were _____ jelly beans left	
2. Megan had 45 blue beads. Katelyn had 41 red beads. How many did they have altogether? They had _____ beads altogether.	

C. Circle the missing sign.

16 ◯ 24 = 40	+ — =

Name _____

Math Test:
Addition and Subtraction with Regrouping

A. Add or subtract the following.

1. 27 − 19	2. 36 +59	3. 92 − 78	4. 83 − 47	5. 39 + 43
6. 44 − 15	7. 56 +37	8. 18 + 67	9. 57 +27	10. 61 − 17

B. Solve the following problems.

Show your work.

1. There were 76 birds on a tree. 18 birds flew away. How many birds were left on the tree? There were _____ birds left.	
2. There were 27 girls and 26 boys playing in the school yard. How many children were playing altogether? _____ children were playing.	

C. Circle the missing sign.

67 ◯ 29 = 96	+ — =

Multiplication Test- Facts 1-5

A. Write a multiplication sentence for each picture.

1.	2.	3.
_____	_____	_____

B. Multiply.

4. 2X5=	5. 10X1=	6. 4X4=
7. 9X3=	8. 3X4=	9. 10 X3=
10. 7X4=	11. 1X1=	12. 9X5=
13. 3X1=	14. 5X3=	15. 8X2=
16. 6X4=	17. 7X5=	18. 8X4=
19. 4X2=	20. 6X2=	21. 3X3=
22. 8X5=	23. 5X5=	24. 6X1=
25. 10X5=	26. 4X3=	27. 2X2=
28. 3X5=	29. 2X1=	30. 5X6=

Multiplication Test- Facts 6-10

A. Write a multiplication sentence for each picture.

1.	2.	3.
_____	_____	_____

B. Multiply.

4. $2 \times 6 =$	5. $4 \times 9 =$	6. $10 \times 8 =$
7. $9 \times 7 =$	8. $10 \times 9 =$	9. $3 \times 6 =$
10. $7 \times 9 =$	11. $9 \times 6 =$	12. $1 \times 10 =$
13. $3 \times 10 =$	14. $8 \times 9 =$	15. $5 \times 7 =$
16. $6 \times 8 =$	17. $7 \times 8 =$	18. $7 \times 6 =$
19. $4 \times 7 =$	20. $3 \times 9 =$	21. $6 \times 10 =$
22. $8 \times 8 =$	23. $6 \times 6 =$	24. $5 \times 9 =$
25. $10 \times 7 =$	26. $2 \times 8 =$	27. $4 \times 10 =$
28. $7 \times 7 =$	29. $6 \times 7 =$	30. $10 \times 9 =$

Division Test Facts 1-5

A. Write a division sentence for each picture.

1.	2.	3.
_____	_____	_____

B. Multiply.

4. $20 \div 5 =$	5. $50 \div 5 =$	6. $45 \div 5 =$
7. $9 \div 3 =$	8. $27 \div 3 =$	9. $18 \div 3 =$
10. $16 \div 4 =$	11. $36 \div 4 =$	12. $32 \div 4 =$
13. $3 \div 1 =$	14. $18 \div 2 =$	15. $8 \div 4 =$
16. $4 \div 2 =$	17. $2 \div 2 =$	18. $8 \div 2 =$
19. $15 \div 5 =$	20. $25 \div 5 =$	21. $35 \div 5 =$
22. $12 \div 3 =$	23. $21 \div 3 =$	24. $27 \div 9 =$
25. $16 \div 4 =$	26. $28 \div 4 =$	27. $36 \div 9 =$
28. $1 \div 1 =$	29. $5 \div 1 =$	30. $4 \div 1 =$

Name _____

Division Test Facts 6-10

A. Write a division sentence for each picture.

1.	2.	3.
_____	_____	_____

B. Divide.

4. $36 \div 6 =$	5. $27 \div 9 =$	6. $100 \div 10 =$
7. $72 \div 8 =$	8. $48 \div 8 =$	9. $90 \div 9 =$
10. $64 \div 8 =$	11. $35 \div 7 =$	12. $40 \div 8 =$
13. $18 \div 9 =$	14. $54 \div 6 =$	15. $56 \div 7 =$
16. $40 \div 10 =$	17. $10 \div 10 =$	18. $42 \div 6 =$
19. $50 \div 10 =$	20. $72 \div 9 =$	21. $49 \div 7 =$
22. $81 \div 9 =$	23. $24 \div 8 =$	24. $16 \div 8 =$
25. $32 \div 8 =$	26. $28 \div 7 =$	27. $9 \div 9 =$
28. $21 \div 7 =$	29. $48 \div 6 =$	30. $70 \div 10 =$

Math Test: Number Words

Match the correct numeral to each number word.

1	eight
2	ten
3	five
4	seven
5	four
6	nine
7	three
8	one
9	six
10	two

Math Test: Number Words

Match the correct numeral to each number word.

11	**twenty**
12	**thirteen**
13	**sixteen**
14	**nineteen**
15	**seventeen**
16	**eighteen**
17	**fourteen**
18	**fifteen**
19	**twelve**
20	**eleven**

Name _____

Math Test: Numbers 1-10

A. How many?

1. _____	2. _____
3. _____	4. _____

B. Count from 1 to 10.

1				
				10

C. Fill in the missing numbers.

5. just after 7, 8, _____	6. between 8, _____, 10
7. just before and after _____, 3, _____	8. just before _____, 7, 8
9. just after 1, 2, _____	10. between 4, _____, 6

Grade 1 Math Test: Numbers 1-10

A. Draw a picture to match each numeral.

nine 9	six 6
seven 7	three 3
four 4	two 2
five 5	eight 8
one 1	ten 10

Grade 1 Math Test: Comparing Sets

A. Look at the pictures.

Draw the pictures to make **more**, **less** or the **same**.

5	more	less	same

4	more	less	same

2	more	less	same

7	more	less	same

Grade 1 Math Test: Counting

A. Fill in the missing numbers.

1. Count backwards by 1's.

   20, 19, _____, _____, _____, _____, _____

2. Count forward by 5's.

   40, 45, _____, _____, _____, _____, _____

3. Count forward by 2's

   56, 58, _____, _____, _____, _____, _____, _____

4. Count forward by 10's

   10, 20, _____, _____, _____, _____, _____, _____

5. Count forward by 1's

   78, 79, _____, _____, _____, _____, _____, _____

6. Count forward by 5's.

   55, _____, _____, _____, _____, _____, _____

7. Count forward by 10's

   40, _____, _____, _____, _____, _____,

8. Count forward by 2's

   74, _____ _____, _____, _____, _____, _____

Grade 2 Math Test: Counting

A. Fill in the missing numbers.

1. Count backwards by 1's.

   30, 29, _____, _____, _____, _____ , _____

2. Count forward by 5's.

   125, 130, _____, _____, _____, _____ , _____

3. Count forward by 2's

   125, 127, _____ , _____, _____, _____, _____

4. Count forward by 10's

   150, 160, _____, _____, _____, _____, _____

5. Count forward by 1's

   284, 285, _____, _____, _____, _____, _____

6. Count backwards by 5's.

   275, _____, _____, _____, _____, _____ , _____

7. Count forward by 10's

   110, _____, _____, _____, _____, _____,

8. Count forward by 2's

   174, _____ _____, _____, _____, _____, _____

Name _____

Grade 3 Math Test: Counting

A. Fill in the missing numbers.

1.	Count backwards by 10's. 420, _____, _____, _____, _____ , _____ , _____
2.	Count forward by 5's. 155, _____, _____, _____, _____ ,_____ , _____
3.	Count forward by 2's 672, _____ , _____, _____, _____ ,_____ , _____
4.	Count forward by 10's 890, _____, _____, _____, _____, _____, _____
5.	Count forward by 25's 200, _____, _____, _____, _____, _____ , _____
6.	Count forward by 100's. 200, _____, _____, _____, _____, _____ ,_____
7.	Count backwards by 10's 90, _____, _____, _____, _____, _____, _____
8.	Count forward by 2's 64, _____, _____, _____, _____, _____, _____

Name _____

Math Test: Counting to 100

A. Fill in the numbers on the hundred chart.

1									
									100

Math Test: Place Value Grade 1

A. Write the number.

1. tens _____ ones _____ = _____

2. tens _____ ones _____ = _____

3. tens _____ ones _____ = _____

4. tens _____ ones _____ = _____

5. tens _____ ones _____ = _____

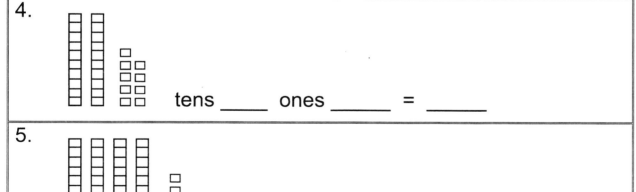

6. 1 ten and 7 ones = _____   7. 4 tens and 5 ones = _____

8. 5 tens and 3 ones = _____   9. 9 tens and 2 ones = _____

10. 7 tens and 9 ones = _____

Number Correct:

_____
10

Grade 2 Math Test: Number Sense

A. Fill in the missing numbers.

1. just after

   39, 40, _____

2. between

   19, _____, 21

3. just before and after

   _____, 98, _____

4. just before

   _____, 54, 55

5. just after

   61, 62, _____

6. between

   64, _____, 66

B. Circle the larger number.

7.   93   17

8.   40   24

9.   82   72

10.   69   33

C. Order each group of numbers from smallest to largest.

11.   91, 45, 39   _____, _____, _____

12.   27, 52, 1   _____, _____, _____

D. Circle to show if the number is odd or even.

13.   33   odd   even

14.   74   odd   even

15.   18   odd   even

16.   50   odd   even

Name _____

Grade 2 Math Test: Place Value

A. Count, then write the base ten names.

1.	_____ hundreds _____ tens _____ ones = _____
2.	_____ hundreds _____ tens _____ ones = _____
3.	_____ hundreds _____ tens _____ones = _____
4.	_____ hundreds _____ tens _____ ones = _____
5.	_____ hundreds _____ tens _____ ones = _____

Grade 2 Math Test: Number Sense

Circle the letter next to the correct answer.

1. What number comes next? 44, 45, 46, _____ A. 37 B. 47 C. 48	2. Which number is 3 less than 26? A. 23 B. 35 C. 62
3. Which number is odd? A. 5 B. 6 C. 10	4. Which creature is first in the row? A. B. C.
5. How many tens in 45? A. 5 tens B. 4 tens C. 3 tens	6. Find the number that is 1 more than 78. A. 80 B. 79 C. 77
7. Eleven is the number word for: A. 17 B. 1 C. 11	8. What number is 10 less than 30? A. 10 B. 20 C. 30
9. Name the numeral for twenty. A. 20 B. 10 C. 15	10. What is 341 in expanded form? A. 300 + 41 B. 30 + 40 +1 C. 300 + 40 + 1

Name _____

Grade 2 Math Test: Number Sense

Circle the letter next to the correct answer.

11. Which number is the greatest? A. 56 B. 100 C. 74	12. Which number is even? A. 604 B. 351 C. 783
13. Which number equals: $$300 + 50 + 2$$ A. 352 B. 325 C. 3052	14. Which creature is sixth in the row? A. B. C.
15. Which is the number word for 12? A. twelve B. thirteen C. twenty	16. What is the missing number? 30, 32, 34, _____, 38, 40 A. 35 B. 36 C. 34
17. How many tens and ones in 98? A. 9 tens and 8 ones B. 8 tens and 9 ones C. 7 tens and 8 ones	18. What number is 10 less than 18? A. 28 B. 10 C. 8
19. Which number is odd? A. 28 B. 30 C. 19	20. What two numbers come next when counting by 10's? 30, 40, 50, ____, ____ A. 30, 40 B. 60, 70 C. 100, 200

Grade 2 Math Test: Number Sense

Circle the letter next to the correct answer.

21. Find the missing sign. 22 ◯ 22 A. < B. = C. >	22. Which number is even? A. 89 B. 60 C. 51
23. Name the numeral for: 300 + 50 +9 A. 359 B. 395 C. 593	24. Which creature is third in the row? A. B. C.
25. Find the missing sign. 67 ◯ 55 A. < B. = C. >	26. How many tens in 671? A. 7 tens B. 1 tens C. 6 tens
27. What is the number word for 684? A. six hundred eighty fourteen B. six hundred eighty-four C. six thousand eighty-four	28. Find the missing sign. 39 ◯ 12 A. < B. = C. >
29. Name the numeral for : 200 + 40 + 2 A. 24 B. 420 C. 242	30. What is 632 in expanded form? A. 60 +32 B. 6 + 300 +2 C. 600 + 30 +2

Grade 3 Math Test: Number Sense

Circle the letter next to the correct answer.

1. Which number is the greatest? A. 604 B. 351 C. 783	2. Which number is the least? A. 787 B. 674 C. 500
3. Which number is odd? A. 787 B. 674 C. 500	4. Which creature is third in the row? A. B. C.
5. How many tens in 6785? A. 7 B. 80 C. 8	6. Which number would be rounded to 800? A. 604 B. 351 C. 783
7. Seventy is the number word for: A. 80 B. 70 C. 60	8. What number is 10 less than 59? A. 29 B. 39 C. 49
9. Name the numeral for: three thousand six hundred five A. 3605 B. 4605 C. 4000	10. What is 6734 in expanded form? A. 6000 +7 + 34 B. 6000 +700 +30 + 4 C. 6000+70 + 30 +4

Grade 3 Math Test: Number Sense

Circle the letter next to the correct answer.

11. Find the missing sign. 786 ◯ 680 A. < B. = C. >	12. Which number is even? A. 342 B. 351 C. 783
13. Which number equals: 6000+ 500+90 +1 ? A. 60 591 B. 65 901 C. 6591	14. Which creature is first in the row? A. B. C.
15. Find the missing sign. 445 ◯ 892 A. < B. = C. >	16. Which number has 9 in the ones place and 8 in the thousand place? A. 86129 B. 68129 C. 48897
17. What is the number word for 489? A. four hundred eight nine B. four hundred eighteen nine C. four hundred eighty nine	18. Find the missing sign. 522 ◯ 522 A. < B. = C. >
19. Name the numeral for : 50 000 + 5000 + 500 + 50 +2 A. 55 5552 B. 55 552 C. 55 52	20. What is 32 866 in expanded form? A. 30 000 + 2000 + 800 + 60 + 6 B. 3000 + 2000 + 800 + 66 C. 32 000 + 800 + 60 + 6

Name _____

Math Test: Fractions

A. What fraction does the shaded part show?

1. $\frac{1}{2}$ $\frac{1}{3}$ $\frac{1}{4}$	2. $\frac{1}{2}$ $\frac{1}{3}$ $\frac{1}{4}$	
3. $\frac{1}{2}$ $\frac{1}{3}$ $\frac{1}{4}$	4. $\frac{1}{2}$ $\frac{1}{3}$ $\frac{1}{4}$	
5. $\frac{1}{2}$ $\frac{1}{3}$ $\frac{1}{4}$	6. $\frac{1}{2}$ $\frac{1}{3}$ $\frac{1}{4}$	
7. $\frac{1}{2}$ $\frac{1}{3}$ $\frac{1}{4}$	8. $\frac{1}{2}$ $\frac{1}{3}$ $\frac{1}{4}$	
9.  $\frac{1}{2}$ $\frac{1}{3}$ $\frac{1}{4}$	10. $\frac{1}{2}$ $\frac{1}{3}$ $\frac{1}{4}$	

Name _____

Math Test: Fractions

A. Circle parts of a group.

1. Circle $\frac{1}{2}$ of the group. 	2. Circle $\frac{1}{2}$ of the group. 
3. Circle $\frac{1}{3}$ of the group. 	4. Circle $\frac{1}{4}$ of the group. 
5. Circle $\frac{1}{2}$ of the group. 	6. Circle $\frac{1}{3}$ of the group. 
7. Circle $\frac{1}{4}$ of the group.	8. Circle $\frac{1}{3}$ of the group.
9. Circle $\frac{1}{2}$ of the group. 	10. Circle $\frac{1}{4}$ of the group. 

Math Test: Coins

A. Match the correct value to each coin.

1.	$1.00
2.	$0.05
3.	$0.01
4.	$2.00
5.	$0.10
6.	$0.25

B. Write the following coin amount in cents.

7. $0.10 _____

8. $0.25 _____

9. $0.05 _____

10. $0.01 _____

Grade 1 Math Test: How much money?

A. What is the total value of each amount of coins?

1.		
2.		
3.		
4.		
5.		
6.		
7.		
8.		
9.		
10.		

Grade 2 Math Test: How much money?

A. What is the total value of each amount of coins?

1.	
2.	
3.	
4.	
5.	
6.	
7.	
8.	
9.	
10.	

Name _____

Grade 3 Math Test: How much money?

A. What is the value of each amount of coins?

1.	
2.	
3.	
4.	
5.	
6.	
7.	
8.	
9.	
10.	

Math Test: What are the coins?

A. Count. What is the value of the coins?

1. Draw 85¢ using 6 coins.

2. Draw 12¢ using 3 coins.

3. Draw 40¢ using 5 coins.

4. Draw 52¢ using 4 coins.

5. Draw 100¢ using 1 coin.

Math Test: What are the coins?

A. Count. What is the value of the coins?

1. Draw $2.30 using 6 coins.

2. Draw $5.64 using 12 coins.

3. Draw $2.84 using 9 coins.

4. Draw $4.57 using 9 coins.

5. Draw $8.92 using 11 coins.

Grade 1 Math Test: Coin Addition

A. Add. What is the value of the coins?

1. How much altogether?

 + =

2. How much altogether?

  + =

3. How much altogether?

  + =

4. How much altogether?

 +   =

5. How much altogether?

   + =

Name _____

Grade 1 Math Test: Coin Subtraction

A. Subtract. What is the value of the coins?

1. How much is left?

 - = _____¢

2. How much is left?

   - = _____¢

3. How much is left?

   - = _____¢

4. How much is left?

  -   = _____¢

5. How much is left?

     - = _____¢

Name _____

Grade 2 Math Test: Coin Addition

A. Add. What is the value of the coins?

Show your work.

1. How much altogether?

   **+** = _____

2. How much altogether?

      **+** = _____

3. How much altogether?

     + = _____

4. How much altogether?

    + = _____

5. How much altogether?

      + = _____

Name _____

Grade 2 Math Test: Coin Subtraction

A. Subtract. What is the value of the coins?

Show your work.

1. How much is left? **-** **=** _____¢	
2. How much is left? **-**  **=** _____¢	
3. How much is left? **-** **=** _____¢	
4. How much is left? **-** 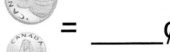 **=** _____¢	
5. How much is left? **-**  **=** _____¢	

Measurement

Tests

Math Test: Telling Time to the Hour #1

A. Write the time in two ways.

1.	2.	3.	4.
____ : ____	____ : ____	____ : ____	____ : ____
___ o'clock	___ o'clock	___ o'clock	___ o'clock
5.	6.	7.	8.
____ : ____	____ : ____	____ : ____	____ : ____
___ o'clock	___ o'clock	___ o'clock	___ o'clock
9.	10.	11.	12.
____ : ____	____ : ____	____ : ____	____ : ____
___ o'clock	___ o'clock	___ o'clock	___ o'clock

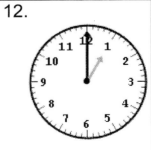

Math Test: Telling Time to the Hour #2

A. Write the time in two ways.

1.	2.	3.	4.

_____ : _____

___ o'clock

_____ : _____

___ o'clock

_____ : _____

___ o'clock

_____ : _____

___ o'clock

5.	6.	7.	8.

_____ : _____

___ o'clock

_____ : _____

___ o'clock

_____ : _____

___ o'clock

_____ : _____

___ o'clock

9.	10.	11.	12.

_____ : _____

___ o'clock

_____ : _____

___ o'clock

_____ : _____

___ o'clock

_____ : _____

___ o'clock

Name _____

Math Test: Telling Time to the Half Hour #1

A. Write the time in two ways.

1.	2.	3.	4.
_____ : _____	_____ : _____	_____ : _____	_____ : _____
half past____	half past____	half past____	half past____

5.	6.	7.	8.
_____ : _____	_____ : _____	_____ : _____	_____ : _____
half past____	half past____	half past____	half past____

9.	10.	11.	12.
_____ : _____	_____ : _____	_____ : _____	_____ : _____
half past____	half past____	half past____	half past____

Math Test: Telling Time to the Half Hour #2

A. Write the time in two ways.

1.  ____ : ____ half past____	2.  ____ : ____ half past____	3.  ____ : ____ half past____	4.  ____ : ____ half past____
5.  ____ : ____ half past____	6.  ____ : ____ half past____	7.  ____ : ____ half past____	8.  ____ : ____ half past____
9.  ____ : ____ half past____	10.  ____ : ____ half past____	11.  ____ : ____ half past____	12.  ____ : ____ half past____

Name _____

Math Test: Telling Time to the Quarter Hour #1

A. Write the time in two ways.

1. 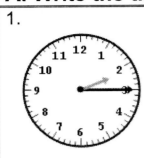 _____ : _____ **quarter past___**	2.  _____ : _____ **quarter past___**	3  _____ : _____ **quarter past___**	4.  _____ : _____ **quarter past___**
5  _____ : _____ **quarter past___**	6  _____ : _____ **quarter past___**	7  _____ : _____ **quarter past___**	8. 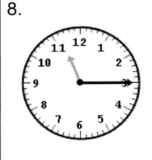 _____ : _____ **quarter past___**
9.  _____ : _____ **quarter past___**	10.  _____ : _____ **quarter past___**	11.  _____ : _____ **quarter past___**	12.  _____ : _____ **quarter past___**

Math Test: Telling Time to the Quarter Hour #2

A. Write the time in two ways.

1	2	3.	4
_____ : _____	_____ : _____	_____ : _____	_____ : _____
quarter past___	quarter past___	quarter past___	quarter past___

5.	6.	7.	8.
_____ : _____	_____ : _____	_____ : _____	_____ : _____
quarter past___	quarter past___	quarter past___	quarter past___

9	10.	11.	12.
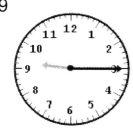		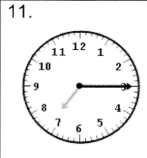	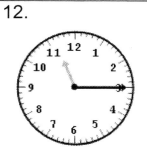
_____ : _____	_____ : _____	_____ : _____	_____ : _____
quarter past___	quarter past___	quarter past___	quarter past___

Name _____

Math Test: Telling Time to the Quarter Hour #3

A. Write the time in two ways.

1.

_____ : _____

quarter to ___

2.

_____ : _____

quarter to ___

3.

_____ : _____

quarter to ___

4.

_____ : _____

quarter to ___

5.

_____ : _____

quarter to ___

6.

_____ : _____

quarter to ___

7.

_____ : _____

quarter to ___

8.

_____ : _____

quarter to ___

9.

_____ : _____

quarter to ___

10.

_____ : _____

quarter to ___

11.

_____ : _____

quarter to ___

12.

_____ : _____

quarter to ___

Math Test: Telling Time to the Quarter Hour #4

A. Write the time in two ways.

1. 	2. 	3. 	4.
_____ : _____	_____ : _____	_____ : _____	_____ : _____
quarter to ___	quarter to ___	quarter to ___	quarter to ___
5. 	6. 	7. 	8. 
_____ : _____	_____ : _____	_____ : _____	_____ : _____
quarter to ___	quarter to ___	quarter to ___	quarter to ___
9. 	10. 	11. 	12.
_____ : _____	_____ : _____	_____ : _____	_____ : _____
quarter to ___	quarter to ___	quarter to ___	quarter to ___

Name _____

Math Test: Telling Time

A. Write the time.

1. 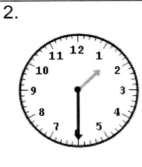 ____:____	2. 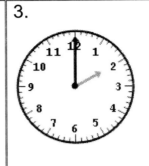 ____:____	3. 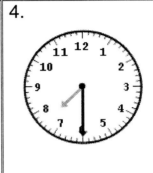 ____:____	4. ____:____
5. ____:____	6.  ____:____	7.  ____:____	8. 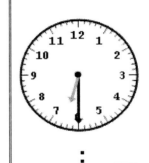 ____:____
9. ____:____	10.  ____:____	11.  ____:____	12. 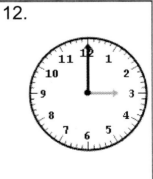 ____:____

Math Test: Telling Time

A. Write the time.

1.

_____ : _____

2.

_____ : _____

3.

_____ : _____

4.

_____ : _____

5.

_____ : _____

6.

_____ : _____

7.

_____ : _____

8.

_____ : _____

9.

_____ : _____

10.

_____ : _____

11.

_____ : _____

12.

_____ : _____

Math Test: Telling Time

A. Write the time.

1.  ____ : ____	2.  ____ : ____	3.  ____ : ____	4. ____ : ____
5.  ____ : ____	6.  ____ : ____	7.  ____ : ____	8.  ____ : ____
9.  ____ : ____	10.  ____ : ____	11.  ____ : ____	12. 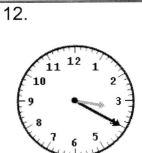 ____ : ____

Math Test: Elapsed Time

A. What is the elapsed time?

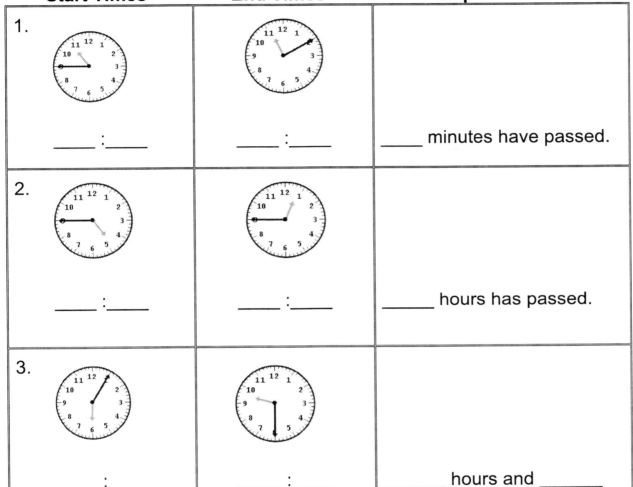

Start Times	End Times	Elapsed Times
1.		
_____ : _____	_____ : _____	_____ minutes have passed.
2.		
_____ : _____	_____ : _____	_____ hours has passed.
3.		
_____ : _____	_____ : _____	_____ hours and _____ minutes have passed.

B. Solve.

4. Ben left for his soccer game at:	Ben was at his soccer game for for 2 hours and 10 minutes.
_____ : _____	What time did Ben return home?

Math Test: Time

Circle the letter next to the correct answer.

1. How many minutes in an hour? A. 10 minutes B. 60 minutes C. 90 minutes	2. How many days in 4 weeks? A. 28 days B. 30 days C. 21 days
3. What is another way to say 9:00? A. 9 o'clock B. quarter to 9 C. half past 9	4. Each week Spencer plays hockey for 100 minutes. How many hours and minutes does he play hockey? A. 1 hour 40 minutes B. 1 hour 30 minutes C. 1 hour 20 minutes
5. About how long would it take to brush your teeth? A. 4 minutes B. 4 hours C. 4 days	6. What time was it 30 minutes before? A. 8:30 B. 8:45 C. 9:00
7. How many months in 3 years? A. 24 months B. 36 months C. 48 months	8. What is another way to say 6:15? A. quarter to 6 B. quarter past 6 C. quarter past 6:15
9. The time is 10:30 am. What time will it be in 45 minutes? A. 11:15 am B. 11:00 am C. 10:45 am	10. What time will it be 3 hours later? A. 9:30 B. 8:30 C. 5:30

Math Test: Days of the Week

Circle the letter next to the correct answer.

1. How many days in a week? A. 10 days B. 5 days C. 7 days	2. What day comes after Saturday? A. Monday B. Friday C. Sunday
3. What day of the week comes before Monday? A. Sunday B. Saturday C. Tuesday	4. When do you usually eat lunch? A. night B. afternoon C. morning
5. What day of the week comes before Wednesday? A. Friday B. Saturday C. Tuesday	6. What day of the week comes after Thursday? A. Sunday B. Friday C. Thursday
7. What day of the week is between Tuesday and Thursday? A. Friday B. Thursday C. Wednesday	8. What day of the week comes before Friday? A. Friday B. Saturday C. Thursday
9. What day of the week is after Friday? A. Friday B. Saturday C. Tuesday	10. What day of the week comes after Tuesday? A. Wednesday B. Thursday C. Friday

Math Test: Months of the Year

Circle the letter next to the correct answer.

1. How many months in a year? A. 10 months B. 11 months C. 12 months	2. What month comes after March? A. May B. April C. February
3. What month comes after May? A. August B. April C. June	4. What month comes before June? A. May B. April C. July
5. What is the first month of the year? A. June B. January C. February	6. What month comes after October? A. August B. January C. November
7. What month is between June and August? A. January B. July C. September	8. What month comes before February? A. January B. December C. March
9. What is the last month of the year? A. September B. March C. December	10. What month comes after July? A. September B. August C. February

Math Test: Measurement

Name _____

Circle the letter next to the correct answer.

1. How long is the rectangle?

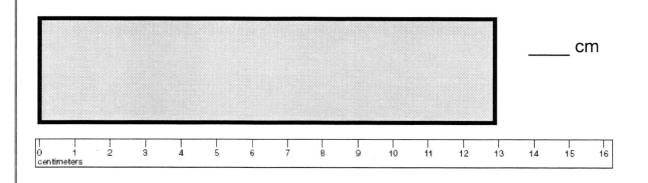

_____ cm

2. How long is the rectangle?

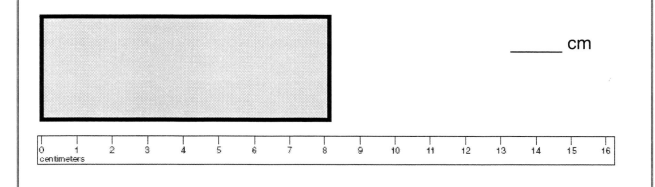

_____ cm

3. How long is the rectangle?

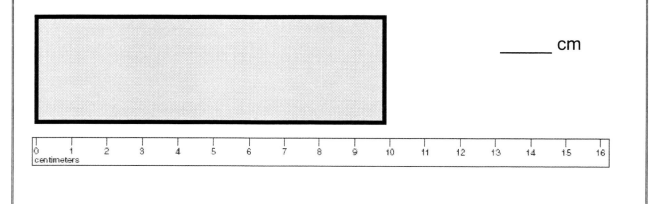

_____ cm

Name _____

Math Test: Measurement

Circle the best measuring tool:

1. to find out the temperature outside

A.   B.   C.

2. to measure the amount of milk in a glass

A.   B.   C.

3. to find out the width of a desk

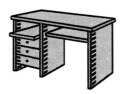

A.   B.   C.

4. to find out the mass of some books

A.   B.   C.

5. to find out the date of a celebration

A.   B.   C.

Math Test: Measurement

Circle the best measuring tool:

6. to know what time to get ready for bedtime

A.   B.   C.

7. to measure the width of your sneaker

A.   B.   C.

8. to find the length of a book

A.   B.   C.

Brain Stretch:
What kind of measuring tools do you use in your daily life?

_____

_____

_____

_____

Math Test: Perimeter

A. Find the perimeters of each figure.

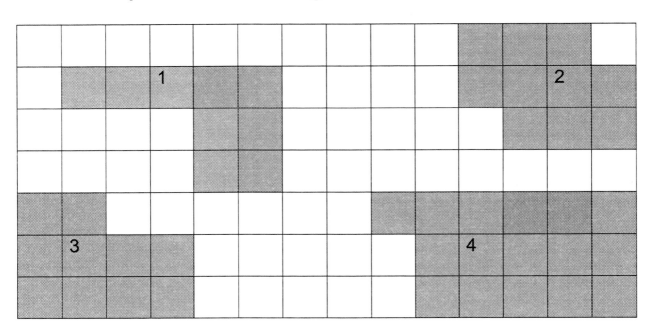

1. The perimeter of figure 1 is: _____units.

2. The perimeter of figure 2 is: _____units.

3. The perimeter of figure 3 is: _____units.

4. The perimeter of figure 4 is: _____units.

B. Solve.

5. Both of these figures have 10 squares.
   Circle the figure with longest perimeter.

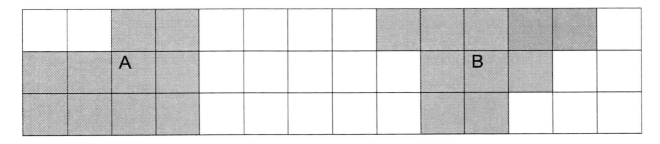

Name _____

Math Test: Area

A. Find the areas of each figure.

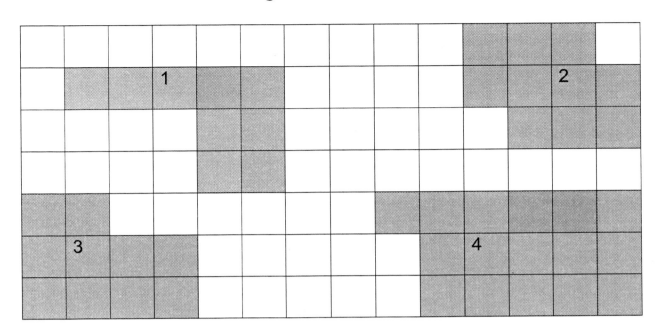

1. The area of figure 1 is: _____units.

2. The area of figure 2 is: _____units.

3. The area of figure 3 is: _____units.

4. The area of figure 4 is: _____units.

B. Solve.

5.   Circle the figure with smallest area.

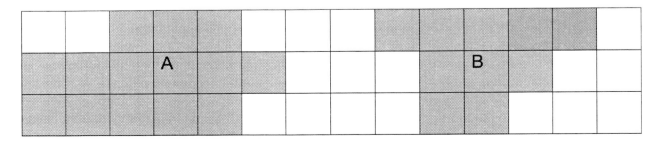

Patterning and Algebra Tests

Math Test: Patterning and Algebra

A. In each row, colour the figures that are the **same shape** and **size**.

1.

2.

B. In each row, colour the shapes to make a pattern.

3.

4.

Math Test: Patterning and Algebra Grade 2

Circle the letter next to the correct answer.

1. What is the pattern rule? 10, 20, 30, 40, 50 A. add 5 B. add 10 C. subtract 10	2. Find the missing number. 32, 34, 36, _____, 40, 42, 44 A. 38 B. 37 C. 39
3. Which number sentence is the same as 4 + 4? A. 2+6 B. 3+6 C. 1+6	4. What are the next two creatures in the pattern? A. B. C.
5. What number comes next? 2, 4, 6, 8, 10, _____ A. 12 B. 11 C. 14	6. What is the pattern rule? 3, 6, 9, 12, _____ A. count by 5's B. count by 10's C. count by 3's
7. What is the next number if the pattern rule is add 5? 12, _____ A. 14 B. 15 C. 17	8. Which number sentence is the same as 10 - 7? A. 6 - 2 B. 5 - 2 C. 4 - 2
9. What is the missing number? _____ - 7 = 4 A. 12 B. 11 C. 10	10. What is the missing number? 6 + _____ = 14 A. 8 B. 7 C. 6

Math Test: Patterning and Algebra Grade 2

Circle the letter next to the correct answer.

11. Find the missing number. 33, 36, _____, 42, 45, 48 A. 38 B. 37 C. 39	12. What is the pattern rule? 50, 40, 30, 20, 10 A. add 5 B. add 10 C. subtract 10
13. What are the next two creatures in the pattern? A. B. C.	14. Which number sentence is the same as 4 + 5? A. 2 + 6 B. 3 + 6 C. 1 + 6
15. What is the pattern rule? 5, 10, 15, 20, 25 A. count by 5's B. count by 10's C. count by 3's	16. What number comes next? 4, 6, 8, 10, 12, _____ A. 12 B. 11 C. 14
17. Which number sentence is the same as 10 - 8? A. 6 - 2 B. 5 - 2 C. 4 - 2	18. What is the next number, if the pattern rule is add 5? 9, _____ A. 14 B. 15 C. 17
19. What is the missing number? 6 + _____ = 13 A. 8 B. 7 C. 6	20. What is the missing number? _____ - 7 = 5 A. 12 B. 11 C. 10

Math Test: Patterning and Algebra Grade 3

Circle the letter next to the correct answer.

1. What is next in the pattern? 30, 60, 90, ____ A. 100 B. 110 C. 120	2. Find the missing number. 222, 224, 226, ____, 230 A. 231 B. 232 C. 228
3. Which number sentence has the same product as 6 X 4? A. 9 X 3 B. 10 X 2 C. 8 X 3	4. What are the next two creatures in the pattern? A. B. C.
5. What number comes next? 1, 3, 5, 7, 9 ____ A. 12 B. 11 C. 14	6 .What is the pattern rule? 10, 20, 40, 80 A. double each time B. multiply by 3 C. add 20
7. What is the next number, if the pattern rule is multiply 5? 7, ____ A. 35 B. 12 C. 30	8. Each box holds 9 cookies. How many cookies in 7 boxes? A. 64 cookies B. 63 cookies C. 72 cookies
9. What is the missing number? ____ ÷ 7 = 7 A. 54 B. 49 C. 63	1 0 . Which number sentence has the same quotient as 81 ÷ 9? A. 32 ÷ 4 B. 48 ÷ 8 C. 27 ÷ 3

Math Test: Patterning and Algebra Grade 3

Circle the letter next to the correct answer.

11. Find the missing number.	12. What is next in the pattern?
222, 225, 228, _____, 234	122312231223122
A. 231	A. 132
B. 232	B. 221
C. 229	C. 312

13. What are the next two creatures in the pattern?

A.

B.

C.

14. Which number sentence has the same product as 5 X 4?

A. 9 X 3

B. 10 X 2

C. 8 X 3

15. What is the pattern rule?

4, 8, 12, 16

A. multiply by 4

B. subtract 4

C. add 4

16. What number comes next?

32, 34, 36, 38, 40, __

A. 42

B. 44

C. 45

17. Each vase holds 6 tulips. How many tulips in 10 vases?

A. 50 tulips

B. 60 tulips

C. 16 tulips

18. What is the next number, if the pattern rule is multiply 8?

4, _____

A. 35

B. 32

C. 30

19. Which number sentence has the same product as 3 X 4 ?

A. 2 X 8

B. 2 X 6

C. 2 X 9

20. What is the missing number?

_____ ÷ 8 = 9

A. 54

B. 64

C. 72

GEOMETRY
Tests

Math Test: Naming Shapes

A. Name each shape.

1. _____	2. _____
3. _____	4. _____
5. _____	6. _____
7. _____	8. _____
9. _____	10. _____

rectangle	square	pentagon	circle	hexagon
octagon	triangle	rhombus	parallelogram	trapezoid

Math Test: Classifying and Sorting Shapes

Read the sorting rule.
Circle the shapes that follow each rule.

1. Shapes with more than 4 sides.

2. Shapes with less than 4 sides.

3. Shapes with more than 4 vertices.

4. Shapes with parallel lines.

5. Shapes that are polygons.

Name _____

Math Test: Classifying and Sorting Shapes

Read the sorting rule.
Circle the shapes that follow each rule.

6. Shapes that have right angles.

7. Shapes that are not polygons.

8. Shapes with more than 5 vertices.

9. Shapes that have equal sides.

10. Shapes that are quadrilaterals.

Math Test: 3D Figures

Draw a line to match each 3D figure to an object that matches.

1.    A.

2.    B.

3.    C.

4. 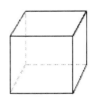   D.

5.   E.

6.    F.

Math Test: 3D Figures

1.

This is a _____.

How many? faces _____ edges _____ vertices _____

2.

This is a _____.

How many? faces _____ edges _____ vertices _____

3.

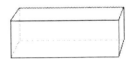

This is a _____.

How many? faces _____ edges _____ vertices _____

4.

This is a _____.

How many? faces _____ edges _____ vertices _____

5.

This is a _____.

How many? faces _____ edges _____ vertices _____

6.

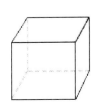

This is a _____.

How many? faces _____ edges _____ vertices _____

Name _____

Math Test: Geometry Grade 2

Circle the letter next to the correct answer.

1. What is the name of this shape?

A. triangle   B. circle   C. rhombus

2. Which figure shows a line of symmetry?

A.   B.   C.

3. What is the name of this 3D figure?

A. cube   B. sphere   C. pyramid

4. What is the name of this shape?

A. pentagon   B. hexagon   C. square

5. Which 3D figure can roll?

A.   B.   C.

6. Look at the shapes. Choose flip, slide or turn.

A. flip   B. slide   C. turn

7. Which shape is a rectangle?

A.   B.   C.

8. What shape has 4 sides?

A. octagon   B. triangle C. square

9. What 3D figure could be made from these pieces?

A. cylinder   B. rectangular C. pyramid
                  prism

10. Which 3D figure is a cube?

A.   B.   C.

Name _____

Math Test: Geometry Grade 2

Circle the letter next to the correct answer.

11. How many faces? A. 5 B. 6 C. 7	12. What is the name of this shape? A. circle B. triangle C. square
13. Which 3D figure can be stacked? A. B. C.	14. Look at the shapes. Choose flip, slide or turn. A. flip B. slide C. turn
15. Which shape does not have a line of symmetry? A. B. C.	16. Which shape does <u>not</u> show a line of symmetry? A. B. C.
17. What 3D figure does this object look like?  A. rectangular prism B. sphere C. pyramid	18. What is the name of this shape?  A. square B. rectangle C. hexagon
19. How many sides does a hexagon have? A. 4 B. 5 C. 6	20. Which 3D figure is a cone? A. B. C.

Math Test: Geometry Grade 3

Circle the letter next to the correct answer.

1. Which figure does not show a line of symmetry? A. B. C.	2. A quadrilateral is a polygon with how many sides? A. 5 sides B. 6 sides C. 4 sides
3. What is the name of the polygon with six sides? A. hexagon B. pentagon C. circle	4. What is the name of this 3D figure? A. cube B. sphere C. pyramid
5. Look at the shapes. Choose flip, slide or turn. 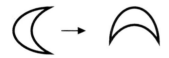 A. flip B. slide C. turn	6. Which 3D figure **cannot** be stacked? A. B. C.
7. How many edges? A. 10 B. 11 C. 12	8. Which shape is an octagon? A. B. C.
9. How many faces? A. 3 B. 2 C. 1	10. What 3D figure could be made from this net? 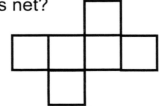 A. cylinder B. cube C. pyramid

Name _____

Math Test: Geometry Grade 3

Circle the letter next to the correct answer.

11. How many vertices does a hexagon have? A. 5 B. 6 C. 7	12. Classify the following pair of lines. 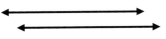 A. parallel B. intersecting C. perpendicular
13. What 3D figure does this object look like? A. cube B. sphere C. cylinder	14. Which pair of shapes look congruent? 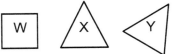 A. W and X B. X and Y C. W and Z
15. Which shape has more than 2 lines of symmetry? A. B. C.	16. Which figures shows a line of symmetry? A. B. C.
17. Which shape is not a quadrilateral? A. rhombus B. square C. hexagon	18. What is the name of this shape? A. square B. trapezoid C. hexagon
19. Which letter has a line of symmetry? A. Y B. K C. R	20. Classify the following pair of lines. A. parallel B. intersecting C. perpendicular

Data Management Tests

Name _____

Math Test: Reading Pictographs

Here are the results of a Favourite Fruit Survey.
Use the pictograph to answer the questions about the results.

Favourite Fruits

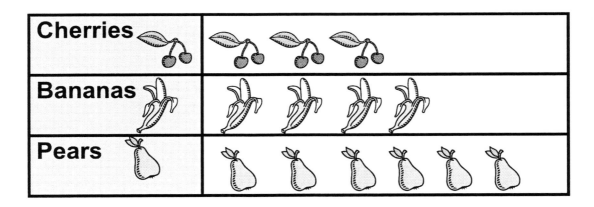

1. How many students chose ? _____

2. How many students chose ? _____

3. Circle the fruit students chose the **most**.

4. Circle the fruit students chose the **least**.

5. How many people voted? _____

Math Test: Reading Pictographs

Here are the results of a Favourite Drink Survey.
Use the pictograph to answer the questions about the results.

Favourite Drinks

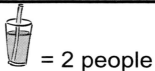 = 2 people

1. What drink do people like the most? _____

2. What drink do people like the least? _____

3. How many people chose milk? _____

4. How many people chose orange juice? _____

5. How many people chose lemonade? _____

6. How many people voted in this survey? _____

7. How many more people chose lemonade than milk? _____

8. How many people chose either orange juice or milk? _____

Math Test: Reading Tally Charts

Here are the results of a Favourite Colour Survey.
Complete the chart and answer the questions about the results.

Colour	Tally	Number
Red	̶H̶H̶T̶ II	
Blue	̶H̶H̶T̶ ̶H̶H̶T̶ III	
Green	IIII	
Purple	̶H̶H̶T̶ III	

1. What was the most popular colour?   _____

2. What was the least popular colour?   _____

3. How many people liked either green or purple?_____

4. How many people took part in the survey? _____

5. How many more people liked blue than red? _____

6. List the colours from the **most** popular to the **least** popular.

1. _____   2. _____

3. _____   4. _____

Math Test: Reading Bar Graphs

Answer the questions using the information from the bar graph.

Favourite Ice Cream Flavours

y-axis

Number of Votes	20
	18
	16
	14
	12
	10
	8
	6
	4
	2

Vanilla   Chocolate   Strawberry   Rocky Road   Other

x-axis

Types of Ice Cream Flavours

1. What is this graph about? _____

2. What is the scale? _____

3. Which flavour was the most popular? _____

4. Which flavour was the least popular? _____

5. How many kids liked strawberry? _____

6. How many kids like either vanilla or chocolate? _____

7. How many people voted altogether? Show your work.

Name _____

Math Test: Constructing Bar Graphs

A. Use the data from the tally chart to make a bar graph. Make sure you label!

Subject	Tally	Number
Reading	卌 IIII	
Math	卌 II	
Art	卌 II	
Science	IIII	

Title _____

10								
9								
8								
7								
6								
5								
4								
3								
2								
1								

_____

Write two things you know from the graph.

1. _____

2. _____

Math Test: Constructing Bar Graphs

A. Use the data from the tally chart to make a bar graph. Make sure you label!

Pet	Tally	Number
Dog	ЖЖЖ	
Cat	ЖЖ II	
Hamster	IIII	
Bird	Ж II	

Title _____

10								
9								
8								
7								
6								
5								
4								
3								
2								
1								

Write two things you know from the graph.

1.

_____

2.

_____

Math Rubric

	Did I solve it?	Did I show my math work?
Full Speed Ahead!	➤ I got the correct answer independently.	➤ I showed all of the steps to solve the problem. ➤ I wrote math language to explain my thinking.
Keep Going!	➤ I completed the problem independently, but made a few mistakes.	➤ I showed most of the steps to solve the problem. ➤ I used some math language to explain my thinking.
Slow Down!	➤ I tried to do the problem, but I need help.	➤ I showed a few steps to solve the problem. ➤ I used a little math language to explain my thinking.
Stop!	➤ I didn't try the problem.	➤ I did not show my math work.

Anecdotal Observations for _____

Math Focus _____

	Strengths	Weaknesses
Completion of Daily Math Work		
Understanding of Math Concepts		
Application of Skills Taught		
Application of Math Terminology to Explain Ideas		
Attendance to Task		

Math Tests Class Record

Student Name														

Addition Facts 0-12 #1

Name _____

5 +8 = 13	1 +6 = 7	2 +8 = 10	7 +5 = 12	6 +3 = 9	8 +0 = 8	4 +6 = 10
3 +4 = 7	10 +3 = 13	7 +9 = 16	3 +2 = 5	2 +10 = 12	8 +3 = 11	4 +2 = 6
9 +5 = 14	1 +2 = 3	5 +6 = 11	4 +1 = 5	5 +10 = 15	9 +3 = 12	Number Correct: ___/20

Addition Facts 0-12 #3

Name _____

2 +4 = 6	5 +2 = 7	1 +5 = 6	2 +9 = 11	6 +0 = 6	1 +8 = 9	4 +6 = 10
3 +7 = 10	3 +3 = 6	10 +2 = 12	6 +4 = 10	2 +10 = 12	8 +3 = 11	4 +0 = 4
5 +5 = 10	7 +2 = 9	1 +8 = 9	4 +5 = 9	7 +4 = 11	0 +9 = 9	Number Correct: ___/20

Addition Facts 0-12 #2

Name _____

6 +3 = 9	1 +2 = 3	2 +0 = 2	3 +4 = 7	6 +7 = 13	4 +6 = 10	5 +2 = 7
3 +7 = 10	10 +4 = 14	5 +5 = 10	4 +4 = 8	3 +10 = 13	8 +2 = 10	4 +9 = 13
6 +1 = 7	1 +3 = 4	3 +5 = 8	4 +7 = 11	5 +6 = 11	9 +0 = 9	Number Correct: ___/20

Addition Facts 0-12 #4

Name _____

3 +5 = 8	9 +2 = 11	1 +0 = 1	7 +3 = 10	3 +8 = 11	6 +6 = 12	8 +2 = 10
3 +4 = 7	2 +4 = 6	1 +5 = 6	4 +7 = 11	0 +10 = 10	2 +2 = 4	3 +9 = 12
4 +2 = 6	6 +3 = 9	5 +7 = 12	6 +5 = 11	1 +6 = 7	3 +0 = 3	Number Correct: ___/20

Addition Facts 10-20 #1

Name _____

2 +9 = 11	5 +8 = 13	6 +5 = 11	4 +10 = 14	8 +8 = 16	10 +8 = 18	7 +6 = 13
6 +6 = 12	9 +5 = 14	8 +7 = 15	6 +4 = 10	3 +10 = 13	8 +9 = 17	9 +9 = 18
5 +10 = 15	10 +9 = 19	9 +4 = 13	8 +6 = 14	7 +7 = 14	10 +1 = 11	Number Correct: ___/20

Addition Facts 10-20 #3

Name _____

8 +6 = 14	9 +5 = 14	5 +5 = 10	7 +7 = 14	6 +7 = 13	6 +5 = 11	4 +9 = 13
7 +4 = 11	10 +6 = 16	8 +9 = 17	6 +6 = 12	10 +10 = 20	8 +3 = 11	3 +9 = 12
4 +6 = 10	10 +0 = 10	9 +1 = 10	8 +8 = 16	2 +9 = 11	10 +7 = 17	Number Correct: ___/20

Addition Facts 10-20 #2

Name _____

8 +5 = 13	9 +6 = 15	1 +10 = 11	7 +6 = 13	3 +7 = 10	6 +6 = 12	8 +4 = 12
3 +8 = 11	2 +9 = 11	7 +5 = 12	3 +10 = 13	10 +10 = 20	10 +4 = 14	3 +9 = 12
4 +7 = 11	6 +8 = 14	10 +5 = 15	6 +6 = 12	7 +9 = 16	7 +10 = 17	Number Correct: ___/20

Addition Facts 10-20 #4

Name _____

9 +9 = 18	9 +8 = 17	8 +7 = 15	3 +10 = 13	7 +9 = 16	6 +9 = 15	9 +8 = 17
4 +10 = 14	7 +5 = 12	10 +9 = 19	3 +7 = 10	4 +8 = 12	10 +3 = 13	9 +2 = 11
10 +5 = 15	8 +2 = 10	5 +8 = 13	1 +10 = 11	9 +4 = 13	0 +10 = 10	Number Correct: ___/20

Name _____ Double Digit Addition #1

82	92	50	78	65	41	43
+ 64	+ 56	+ 52	+ 11	+ 34	+15	+ 30
146	148	102	89	99	56	73

79	10	33	14	30	82	31
+ 10	+ 63	+ 42	+62	+17	+ 34	+ 90
89	73	75	76	47	116	111

15	22	45	80	42	10	Number Correct:
+ 63	+ 75	+ 54	+ 16	+ 53	+77	
78	97	99	96	95	87	20

Name _____ Double Digit Addition: Regrouping #1

79	31	18	27	16	48	63
+ 12	+ 59	+ 68	+ 53	+ 46	+35	+27
91	90	86	80	62	83	90

19	34	76	15	23	22	39
+ 61	+ 47	+ 17	+ 75	+48	+ 38	+ 13
80	81	93	90	71	60	52

89	45	45	28	35	14	Number Correct:
+ 14	+ 56	+ 47	+ 76	+ 55	+ 77	
103	101	92	104	90	91	20

Name _____ Double Digit Addition #2

12	80	48	73	37	66	18
+ 64	+ 17	+ 61	+ 10	+ 52	+ 93	+ 81
76	97	109	83	89	159	99

49	85	22	33	54	70	62
+ 10	+ 52	+ 66	+ 70	+ 84	+23	+ 14
59	137	88	103	138	93	76

20	49	35	10	24	30	Number Correct:
+ 55	+ 30	+ 84	+ 10	+ 45	+ 10	
75	79	119	20	69	40	20

Name _____ Double Digit Addition: Regrouping #2

12	28	48	73	37	39	18
+ 69	+ 27	+ 36	+ 19	+ 54	+ 13	+ 28
81	55	84	92	91	52	46

49	35	25	33	29	37	66
+ 17	+ 56	+ 66	+ 38	+ 84	+23	+ 14
66	91	91	71	113	60	80

25	49	15	19	27	17	Number Correct:
+ 55	+ 45	+ 88	+ 19	+ 45	+ 27	
80	94	103	38	72	44	20

Name _____ Subtraction Facts 0-12 #1

10	6	11	7	6	8	10
- 8	- 6	- 8	- 5	- 3	- 0	- 6
2	0	3	2	3	8	4

4	10	12	3	2	8	7
- 4	- 3	- 9	- 2	- 1	- 3	- 2
0	7	3	1	1	5	5

7	5	8	4	5	9	Number Correct:
- 5	- 2	- 6	- 1	- 0	- 3	
2	3	2	3	5	6	20

Name _____ Subtraction Facts 0-12 #3

10	11	7	8	6	8	10
- 9	- 7	- 6	- 5	- 3	- 4	- 2
1	4	1	3	3	4	8

4	12	10	3	2	8	7
- 1	- 8	- 4	- 2	- 1	- 3	- 5
3	4	6	1	1	5	2

7	8	5	6	8	9	Number Correct:
- 4	- 2	- 1	- 1	- 0	- 7	
3	6	4	5	8	2	20

Name _____ Subtraction Facts 0-12 #2

9	6	2	3	6	7	5
- 5	- 3	- 2	- 0	- 2	- 6	- 4
4	3	0	3	4	1	1

8	10	12	6	12	8	11
- 4	- 7	- 4	- 5	-10	- 2	- 9
4	3	8	1	2	6	2

7	6	9	8	11	9	Number Correct:
- 4	- 1	- 3	- 5	- 6	- 0	
3	5	6	3	5	9	20

Name _____ Subtraction Facts 0-12 #4

6	9	7	4	5	9	5
- 2	- 9	- 3	- 2	- 0	- 6	- 4
4	0	4	2	5	3	1

10	8	12	12	6	3	11
- 8	- 1	-10	- 9	- 5	- 1	- 9
2	7	2	3	1	2	2

6	12	11	9	8	9	Number Correct:
- 0	- 6	- 2	- 4	- 3	- 0	
6	6	9	5	5	9	20

Subtraction Facts 10-20 #1

12 - 8 4	11 - 6 5	14 - 8 6	16 - 7 9	13 - 9 4	17 - 7 10	10 - 6 4
12 - 4 8	13 - 3 10	12 - 7 5	18 - 9 9	15 - 5 10	11 - 3 8	16 - 9 7
18 - 8 10	20 -10 10	15 - 6 9	10 - 9 1	11 - 9 2	14 - 7 7	Number Correct: ___ 20

Subtraction Facts 10-20 #3

14 - 8 6	13 - 5 8	12 - 3 9	11 - 1 10	16 - 6 10	18 - 9 9	10 -7 3
12 - 7 5	15 - 5 10	12 - 6 6	13 - 5 8	17 - 9 8	11 -10 1	16 - 8 8
15 - 9 6	11 - 6 5	19 - 9 10	20 -10 10	10 - 3 7	14 - 7 7	Number Correct: ___ 20

Subtraction Facts 10-20 #2

11 - 8 3	14 - 6 8	12 - 5 7	16 - 6 10	13 - 4 9	17 - 10 7	10 - 2 8
13 - 6 7	12 - 3 9	12 - 2 10	18 - 7 11	15 - 7 8	11 - 4 7	17 - 9 8
20 - 9 11	15 - 7 8	18 - 9 9	10 - 1 9	11 - 2 9	14 - 4 10	Number Correct: ___ 20

Subtraction Facts 10-20 #4

14 - 5 9	16 - 9 7	11 - 4 7	12 - 7 5	13 - 6 7	17 - 7 10	10 - 5 5
12 - 1 11	19 - 5 14	14 - 5 9	12 - 5 7	15 - 7 8	11 - 8 3	17 - 8 9
15 - 9 6	10 - 0 10	20 - 5 15	18 - 8 10	11 - 4 7	14 - 4 10	Number Correct: ___ 20

Double Digit Subtraction #1

34 - 21 13	72 - 50 22	53 - 23 30	49 - 27 22	38 - 18 20	25 - 24 1	37 - 26 11
56 - 34 22	91 - 10 81	38 - 26 12	89 - 41 48	37 - 12 25	76 - 34 42	65 - 25 40
95 - 32 63	72 - 10 62	64 - 23 41	59 - 28 31	64 - 51 13	33 - 21 12	Number Correct: ___ 20

Double Digit Subtraction with Regrouping #1

97 - 29 68	71 - 69 2	61 - 14 47	49 - 27 22	75 - 26 49	66 - 59 7	81 - 25 56
84 - 77 7	91 - 28 63	31 - 16 15	82 - 45 37	37 - 18 19	66 - 39 27	90 - 29 61
74 - 17 57	72 - 18 54	51 - 23 28	48 - 29 19	60 - 41 19	53 - 28 25	Number Correct: ___ 20

Double Digit Subtraction #2

93 - 73 20	64 - 31 33	82 - 60 22	75 - 40 35	48 - 32 16	35 - 24 11	27 - 15 12
37 - 20 17	39 - 24 15	68 - 52 16	84 - 42 42	32 - 12 20	97 - 34 63	65 - 23 42
48 - 36 12	92 - 30 62	59 - 10 49	89 - 58 31	34 - 31 3	71 - 60 11	Number Correct: ___ 20

Double Digit Subtraction with Regrouping #2

64 - 38 26	82 - 69 13	70 - 46 24	42 - 38 4	97 - 73 24	34 - 25 9	25 - 17 8
44 - 39 5	62 - 55 7	82 - 43 39	50 - 31 19	30 - 26 4	94 - 37 57	73 - 25 48
92 - 30 62	70 - 49 21	88 - 59 29	51 - 34 17	41 - 36 5	70 - 13 57	Number Correct: ___ 20

419	497	827	146	732	336	543
+176	+ 286	+ 155	+ 590	+ 149	+527	+ 257
595	783	982	736	881	863	800

708	837	693	748	406	586	717
+123	+109	+176	+188	+259	+122	+ 244
831	946	869	936	665	708	961

365	260	684	578	791	584	Number Correct:
+472	+295	+ 285	+ 330	+ 165	+ 230	____
837	555	969	908	956	814	20

662	493	821	846	739	936	446
-476	- 286	- 155	- 590	- 249	- 527	- 257
186	207	666	256	490	409	189

708	832	693	518	406	516	717
- 123	-309	-376	-188	- 252	-122	- 243
585	523	317	330	154	394	474

765	260	684	570	791	534	Number Correct:
- 472	- 135	- 285	- 318	- 165	- 280	____
293	125	399	252	626	254	20

290	160	362	628	648	724	788
+130	+ 594	+ 353	+136	+168	+ 419	+ 123
420	754	715	764	816	1143	911

192	507	431	484	642	536	158
+589	+308	+388	+243	+199	+156	+ 619
781	815	819	727	841	692	777

407	665	385	783	453	238	Number Correct:
+399	+119	+ 140	+142	+ 350	+ 257	____
806	784	525	925	803	495	20

290	764	862	628	848	724	680
-139	- 592	- 353	-136	- 163	- 419	- 123
151	172	509	492	685	305	557

692	547	431	484	642	571	958
- 379	- 309	- 308	- 246	- 129	- 256	- 629
313	238	123	238	513	315	329

607	665	380	783	450	938	Number Correct:
- 394	- 129	- 145	- 148	- 153	- 257	____
213	536	235	635	297	681	20

$4.74	$5.83	$9.62	$2.60	$4.63	$1.82	$7.83
+ $2.62	-$1.25	- $7.32	+ $2.79	-$3.14	+ $4.41	-$5.26
$7.36	$4.58	$2.30	$5.39	$1.49	$6.23	$2.57

$8.25	$9.42	$5.60	$4.50	$7.46	$3.00	$9.42
- $2.37	- $4.12	+ $3.75	-$0.50	- $5.12	+ $0.75	- $4.13
$5.88	$5.30	$9.35	$4.00	$2.34	$3.75	$5.29

$5.74	$1.80	$9.66	$1.97	$4.81	$2.18	Number Correct:
+ $3.62	+$5.25	- $3.18	+ $2.06	-$3.22	+ $1.43	____
$9.36	$7.05	$6.48	$4.03	$1.59	$3.61	20

$3.74	$9.02	$4.69	$7.81	$7.23	$4.82	$2.74
+ $5.19	- $3.32	+ $4.79	-$4.55	-$5.19	+ $3.18	+ $2.62
$8.93	$5.70	$9.48	$3.26	$2.04	$8.00	$5.36

$8.25	$1.25	$5.50	$9.42	$7.46	$7.00	$8.28
- $1.58	+ $3.80	-$0.50	- $3.80	- $5.12	+ $0.75	- $1.33
$6.67	$5.05	$5.00	$5.62	$2.34	$7.75	$6.95

$2.84	$9.14	$2.17	$2.80	$4.33	$6.18	Number Correct:
+ $6.62	- $3.08	+ $4.06	+$5.30	-$1.99	+ $3.48	____
$9.46	$6.06	$6.23	$8.10	$2.34	$9.66	20

2	4	5	8	6	10	7
X 5	X 2	X 4	X 1	X 3	X 2	X 3
10	8	20	8	18	20	21

6	6	9	3	3	8	8
X 4	X 3	X 5	X 2	X 4	X 1	X 5
24	18	45	6	12	8	40

1	8	10	7	7	10	Number Correct:
X 4	X 1	X 3	X 5	X 2	X 1	____
4	8	30	35	14	10	20

7	6	3	5	5	8	4
X 4	X 1	X 5	X 2	X 3	X 2	X 3
28	6	15	10	15	16	12

10	9	8	7	1	2	3
X 5	X 2	X 4	X 3	X 4	X 1	X 4
50	18	32	21	4	2	12

3	6	4	5	8	3	Number Correct:
X 3	X 5	X 4	X 1	X 2	X 1	____
9	30	16	5	16	3	20

Multiplication Facts 6-10   #1

Name _____

8 X 7 = 56	2 X 6 = 12	4 X 10 = 40	5 X 8 = 40	6 X 9 = 54	10 x 10 = 100	1 X 6 = 6
3 X 10 = 30	4 X 7 = 28	6 X 8 = 48	9 X 9 = 81	2 X 8 = 16	8 X 6 = 48	8 X 9 = 72
7 X 6 = 42	1 X 9 = 9	8 X 8 = 64	10 X 7 = 70	5 X 6 = 30	10 X 9 = 90	Number Correct: ____ 20

Division Facts 1-5   #1

Name _____

10 ÷ 5 = 2	6 ÷ 2 = 3	15 ÷ 5 = 3	18 ÷ 2 = 9	2 ÷ 1 = 2	24 ÷ 4 = 6	25 ÷ 5 = 5
20 ÷ 4 = 5	4 ÷ 1 = 4	9 ÷ 3 = 3	18 ÷ 3 = 6	20 ÷ 2 = 10	28 ÷ 4 = 7	4 ÷ 4 = 1
21 ÷ 3 = 7	10 ÷ 2 = 5	12 ÷ 2 = 6	36 ÷ 4 = 9	27 ÷ 3 = 9	30 ÷ 6 = 5	Number Correct: ____ 20

Multiplication Facts 6-10   #2

Name _____

2 X 7 = 14	4 X 6 = 24	5 X 9 = 45	8 X 3 = 24	9 X 10 = 90	5 x 6 = 30	3 X 7 = 21
9 X 8 = 72	3 X 7 = 21	3 X 9 = 27	8 X10 = 80	1 X 10 = 10	4 X 9 = 36	5 X 8 = 40
6 X 10 = 60	3 X 6 = 18	4 X 8 = 32	7 X 8 = 56	9 X 6 = 54	5 X 7 = 35	Number Correct: ____ 20

Division Facts 1-5   #2

Name _____

8 ÷ 2 = 4	5 ÷ 5 = 1	16 ÷ 2 = 8	12 ÷ 4 = 3	45 ÷ 5 = 9	1 ÷ 1 = 1	30 ÷ 5 = 6
18 ÷ 3 = 6	32 ÷ 4 = 8	7 ÷ 1 = 7	28 ÷ 7 = 4	30 ÷ 3 = 10	14 ÷ 2 = 7	3 ÷ 1 = 3
16 ÷ 4 = 4	12 ÷ 3 = 4	4 ÷ 2 = 4	35 ÷ 5 = 7	40 ÷ 4 = 10	21 ÷ 7 = 3	Number Correct: ____ 20

Chalkboard Publishing ©2006

Division Facts 6-10   #1

Name _____

80 ÷ 10 = 8	35 ÷ 7 = 5	18 ÷ 9 = 2	12 ÷ 6 = 2	45 ÷ 5 = 9	10 ÷ 10 = 1	30 ÷ 10= 3
18 ÷ 9 = 2	32 ÷ 8 = 4	24 ÷ 6 = 4	32 ÷ 4 = 8	35 ÷ 5 = 7	48 ÷ 6 = 8	49 ÷ 7 = 7
63 ÷ 9 = 7	14 ÷ 7 = 2	64 ÷ 8 = 8	30 ÷ 6 = 5	40 ÷10 = 4	45 ÷ 9 = 5	Number Correct: ____ 20

Division Facts 6-10   #1

Name _____

4 ÷ 4 = 1	10 ÷ 10 = 1	35 ÷ 7 = 5	45 ÷ 5 = 9	72 ÷ 8 = 9	16 ÷ 2 = 8	10 ÷ 5 = 2
16 ÷ 4 = 4	9 ÷ 3 = 3	32 ÷ 8 = 4	21 ÷ 3 = 7	42 ÷ 7= 6	48 ÷ 6 = 8	49 ÷ 7= 7
40 ÷ 8= 5	90 ÷ 9 = 10	14 ÷ 2 = 7	30 ÷ 6 = 5	40 ÷10 = 4	72 ÷ 9 = 8	Number Correct: ____ 20

Division Facts 6-10   #2

Name _____

90 ÷ 10 = 9	20 ÷ 10 = 2	6 ÷ 6 = 1	42 ÷ 7 = 6	27 ÷ 9 = 3	40 ÷ 5 = 8	30 ÷ 3 = 10
81 ÷ 9 = 9	72 ÷ 8 = 9	48 ÷ 8 = 6	56 ÷ 8 = 7	36 ÷ 6 = 6	35 ÷ 7 = 5	70 ÷ 7 = 10
72 ÷ 9 = 8	36 ÷ 9 = 4	54 ÷ 6 = 9	28 ÷ 7 = 4	80 ÷ 8 = 10	40 ÷ 4 = 10	Number Correct: ____ 20

Division Facts 1-10   #2

Name _____

20 ÷ 5 = 4	50 ÷ 10 = 5	6 ÷ 6 = 1	27 ÷ 3 = 9	27 ÷ 9 = 3	40 ÷ 5 = 8	3 ÷ 1= 3
81 ÷ 9 = 9	8 ÷ 4 = 32	40 ÷ 4 = 10	56 ÷ 8 = 7	32 ÷ 4 = 8	56 ÷ 7= 8	20 ÷ 2= 10
72 ÷ 9 = 8	6 ÷ 2 = 3	54 ÷ 6 = 9	28 ÷ 7 = 4	8 ÷ 8 = 1	40 ÷ 10 = 4	Number Correct: ____ 20

Chalkboard Publishing ©2006

Addition and Subtraction Facts to 20

A. Add or subtract the following.

1. $\begin{array}{r} 3 \\ +\ 9 \\ \hline 12 \end{array}$	2. $\begin{array}{r} 6 \\ -\ 2 \\ \hline 4 \end{array}$	3. $\begin{array}{r} 4 \\ +\ 4 \\ \hline 8 \end{array}$	4. $\begin{array}{r} 18 \\ -\ 9 \\ \hline 9 \end{array}$	5. $\begin{array}{r} 5 \\ +\ 6 \\ \hline 11 \end{array}$
6. $\begin{array}{r} 13 \\ -\ 7 \\ \hline 6 \end{array}$	7. $\begin{array}{r} 2 \\ +\ 2 \\ \hline 4 \end{array}$	8. $\begin{array}{r} 11 \\ -\ 3 \\ \hline 8 \end{array}$	9. $\begin{array}{r} 2 \\ +\ 8 \\ \hline 10 \end{array}$	10. $\begin{array}{r} 15 \\ -\ 6 \\ \hline 9 \end{array}$

B. Solve the following problems.

	Show your work.
1. There were 12 ants on a log. 6 ants crawled away. How many ants were left on the log? There were ___6___ ants left.	$12 - 6 = 6$
2. There were 7 girls and 6 boys playing hockey. How many children were playing hockey altogether? ___13___ children were playing.	$7 + 6 = 13$

C. Circle the missing sign.

4 ( ) 8 = 12 | (+) — =

Math Test:
Double Digit Addition and Subtraction

A. Add or subtract the following.

1. $\begin{array}{r} 67 \\ -\ 25 \\ \hline 42 \end{array}$	2. $\begin{array}{r} 37 \\ +52 \\ \hline 89 \end{array}$	3. $\begin{array}{r} 82 \\ -\ 41 \\ \hline 41 \end{array}$	4. $\begin{array}{r} 59 \\ -\ 37 \\ \hline 22 \end{array}$	5. $\begin{array}{r} 35 \\ +\ 52 \\ \hline 87 \end{array}$
6. $\begin{array}{r} 25 \\ -\ 14 \\ \hline 11 \end{array}$	7. $\begin{array}{r} 16 \\ +82 \\ \hline 98 \end{array}$	8. $\begin{array}{r} 28 \\ +\ 71 \\ \hline 99 \end{array}$	9. $\begin{array}{r} 57 \\ +20 \\ \hline 77 \end{array}$	10. $\begin{array}{r} 48 \\ -\ 17 \\ \hline 31 \end{array}$

B. Solve the following problems.

	Show your work.
1. There were 67 jelly beans in a jar. 33 of the jelly beans were eaten. How many jelly beans were left in the jar? There were ___34___ jelly beans left	$67 - 33 = 34$
2. Megan had 45 blue beads. Katelyn had 41 red beads. How many did they have altogether? They had ___86___ beads altogether.	$45 + 41 = 86$

C. Circle the missing sign.

16 ( ) 24 = 40 | (+) — =

Math Test:
Addition and Subtraction with Regrouping

A. Add or subtract the following.

1. $\begin{array}{r} 27 \\ -\ 19 \\ \hline 8 \end{array}$	2. $\begin{array}{r} 36 \\ +59 \\ \hline 95 \end{array}$	3. $\begin{array}{r} 92 \\ -\ 78 \\ \hline 14 \end{array}$	4. $\begin{array}{r} 83 \\ -\ 47 \\ \hline 36 \end{array}$	5. $\begin{array}{r} 39 \\ +\ 43 \\ \hline 82 \end{array}$
6. $\begin{array}{r} 44 \\ -\ 15 \\ \hline 29 \end{array}$	7. $\begin{array}{r} 56 \\ +37 \\ \hline 93 \end{array}$	8. $\begin{array}{r} 18 \\ +\ 67 \\ \hline 85 \end{array}$	9. $\begin{array}{r} 57 \\ +27 \\ \hline 84 \end{array}$	10. $\begin{array}{r} 61 \\ -\ 17 \\ \hline 44 \end{array}$

B. Solve the following problems.

	Show your work.
1. There were 76 birds on a tree. 18 birds flew away. How many birds were left on the tree? There were ___58___ birds left.	$76 - 18 = 58$
2. There were 27 girls and 26 boys playing in the school yard. How many children were playing altogether? ___53___ children were playing.	$27 + 26 = 53$

C. Circle the missing sign.

67 ( ) 29 = 99 | (+) — =

Multiplication Test- Facts 1-5

A. Write a multiplication sentence for each picture.

1. ___3 X 4 = 12___	2. ___2 X 3 = 6___	3. ___3 X 2 = 6___

B. Multiply.

4. 2X5= 10	5. 10X1= 10	6. 4X4= 16
7. 9X3= 27	8. 3X4= 12	9. 10 X 3= 30
10. 7X4= 28	11. 1X1= 1	12. 9X5= 45
13. 3X1= 3	14. 5X3= 15	15. 8X2= 16
16. 6X4= 24	17. 7X5= 35	18. 8X4= 32
19. 4X2= 8	20. 6X2= 12	21. 3X3= 9
22. 8X5= 40	23. 5X5= 25	24. 6X1= 6
25. 10X5= 50	26. 4X3= 12	27. 2X2= 4
28. 3X5= 15	29. 2X1= 2	30. 5X6= 30

Multiplication Test- Facts 6-10

A. Write a multiplication sentence for each picture.

1.	2.	3.
2 X 6 = 12	3 X 7 = 21	3 X 9 = 27

B. Multiply.

4. 2X6= 12	5. 4X9= 36	6. 10X8= 80
7. 9X7= 63	8. 10X9= 90	9. 3X6= 18
10. 7X9= 63	11. 9X6= 54	12. 1X10= 10
13. 3X10= 30	14. 8X9= 72	15. 5X7= 35
16. 6X8= 48	17. 7X8= 56	18. 7X6= 42
19. 4X7= 28	20. 3X9= 27	21. 6X10= 60
22. 8X8= 64	23. 6X6= 36	24. 5X9= 45
25. 10X7= 70	26. 2X8= 16	27. 4X10= 40
28. 7X7= 49	29. 6X7= 42	30. 10X9= 90

Chalkboard Publishing ©2006

Division Test Facts 1-5

A. Write a division sentence for each picture.

1.	2.	3.
10 ÷ 2 = 5	8 ÷ 2 = 4	9 ÷ 3 = 3

B. Divide.

4. 20÷5= 4	5. 50÷5= 10	6. 45÷5= 9
7. 9÷3= 3	8. 27÷3= 9	9. 18÷3= 6
10. 16÷4= 4	11. 36÷4= 9	12. 32÷4= 8
13. 3÷1= 3	14. 18÷2= 9	15. 8÷4= 2
16. 4÷2= 2	17. 2÷2= 1	18. 8÷2= 4
19. 15÷5= 3	20. 25÷5= 5	21. 35÷5= 7
22. 12÷3= 4	23. 21÷3= 7	24. 27÷9= 3
25. 16÷4= 4	26. 28÷4= 7	27. 36÷9= 4
28. 1÷1= 1	29. 5÷1= 5	30. 4÷1= 4

Chalkboard Publishing ©2006

Division Test Facts 6-10

A. Write a division sentence for each picture.

1.	2.	3.
18 ÷ 3 = 6	21 ÷ 3 = 7	36 ÷ 4 = 9

B. Divide.

4. 36÷6= 6	5. 27÷9= 3	6. 100÷10= 10
7. 72÷8= 9	8. 48÷8= 6	9. 90÷9= 10
10. 64÷8= 8	11. 35÷7= 5	12. 40÷8= 5
13. 18÷9= 2	14. 54÷6= 9	15. 56÷7= 8
16. 40÷10= 4	17. 10÷10= 1	18. 42÷6= 7
19. 50÷10= 5	20. 72÷9= 8	21. 49÷7= 7
22. 81÷9= 9	23. 24÷8= 3	24. 16÷8= 2
25. 32÷8= 4	26. 28÷7= 4	27. 9÷9= 1
28. 21÷7= 3	29. 48÷6= 8	30. 70÷10= 7

Chalkboard Publishing ©2006

Answer Pages

Page 30 Grade 1 Math Test: Number Words

1 – one	2 – two	3 – three	4 – four	5 – five
6 – six	7 – seven	8 – eight	9 – nine	10 – ten

Page 31 Grade 1 Math Test: Number Words

11 – eleven	12 – twelve	13 – thirteen	14 – fourteen	15 – fifteen
16 – sixteen	17 – seventeen	18 – eighteen	19 – nineteen	20 – twenty

Page 32 Grade 1 Math Test: Numbers 1-10

A.
   1. 6   2. 4   3. 2   4. 8

C.
5.	7, 8, **9**	6.	8, **9**, 10
7.	**2**, 3, **4**	8.	**6**, 7, 8
9.	1, 2, 3	10.	4, **5**, 6

Page 35 Grade 1 Math Test: Counting

1. 20, 19, **18, 17, 16, 15, 14, 13**
2. 40, 45, **50, 55, 60, 65, 70, 75**
3. 56, 58, **60, 62, 64, 66, 68, 70**
4. 10, 20, **30, 40, 50, 60, 70, 80**
5. 78, 79, **80, 81, 82, 83, 84, 85**
6. 55, **50, 45, 40, 35, 30, 25**
7. 40, **50, 60, 70, 80, 90, 100**
8. 74, **76, 78, 80, 82, 84, 88**

Page 36 Grade 2 Math Test: Counting

1. 30, 29, **28, 27, 26, 25, 24, 23**
2. 125, 130, **135, 140, 145, 150, 155**
3. 125, 127, **129, 131, 133, 135, 137**
4. 150, 160, **170, 180, 190, 200, 210**
5. 284, 285, **286, 287, 288, 289, 290**
6. 275, **270, 265, 260, 255, 250, 245**
7. 110, **120, 130, 140, 150, 160, 170**
8. 174, **176, 178, 180, 182, 184, 186**

Page 37 Grade 3 Math Test: Counting

1. 420, **410, 400, 390, 380, 370, 360**
2. 155, **160, 165, 170, 175, 180, 185**
3. 672, **674, 676, 678, 680, 682, 684**
4. 890, **900, 910, 920, 930, 940, 950**
5. 200, **225, 250, 275, 300, 325, 350**
6. 200, **300, 400, 500, 600, 700, 800**
7. 90, 80, 70, 60, 50, 40, 30
8. 64, **66, 68, 70, 72, 74, 76**

Page 39 Math Test: Place Value Grade 1

1. tens 3 ones 6 = 36
2. tens 1 ones 2 = 12
3. tens 1 ones 4 = 14
4. tens 2 ones 9 = 29
5. tens 4 ones 5 = 45
6. 17
7. 45
8. 53
9. 92
10. 79

Page 40   Math Test: Number Sense Grade 2

1. 39, 40, **41**
4. **53**, 54, 55
7. 93
10. 69
13. odd
16. even

2. 19, **20**, 21
5. 61, 62, **63**
8. 40
11. 39, 45, 91
14. odd

3. **97**, 98, **99**
6. 64, **65**, 66
9. 82
12. 1, 27, 52
15. even

Page 41   Math Test: Place Value Grade 2

1. 1 hundreds 5 tens 3 ones = 153
2. 4 hundreds 1 tens 8 ones = 418
3. 2 hundreds 3 tens 4 ones = 234
4. 5 hundreds 4 tens 6 ones = 546
5. 7 hundreds 6 tens 2 ones = 762

Pages 42 - 44   Math Test: Number Sense Grade 2

1. B	2. A.	3. A	4. A	5. B
6. B	7. C	8. B	9. A	10. C
11. B	12. A	13. A	14. B	15. A
16. B	17. A	18. C	19. C	20. B
21. B	22. B	23. A	24. C	25. C
26. A	27. B	28. C	29. C	30. C

Page 45   Math Test: Number Sense Grade 3

1. C	2. C	3. A	4. C	5. C
6. C	7. B	8. C	9. A	10. B

Page 46   Math Test: Number Sense Grade 3

11. C	12. A	13. C	14. C	15. A
16. B	17. C	18. B	19. B	20. A

Page 47   Math Test: Fractions

1. $\frac{1}{3}$
2. $\frac{1}{2}$
3. $\frac{1}{4}$
4. $\frac{1}{3}$
5. $\frac{1}{2}$
6. $\frac{1}{4}$
7. $\frac{1}{4}$
8. $\frac{1}{3}$
9. $\frac{1}{3}$
10. $\frac{1}{2}$

Page 49   Math Test: Coins

7. 10 ¢   8. 25 ¢   9. 5 ¢   10. 1¢

Page 50   Math Test: How much money? Grade 1

1. 18 ¢	2. 20 ¢	3. 14 ¢	4. 11 ¢	5. 8 ¢
6. 18 ¢	7. 16 ¢	8. 20 ¢	9. 20 ¢	10. 20 ¢

Page 51   Math Test: How much money? Grade 2

1. $ 0.52	2. $ 0.56	3. $ 0.50	4. $ 1.00	5. $ 0.26
6. $ 0.42	7. $ 0.70	8. $ 1.01	9. $ 0.59	10. $ 0.61

Page 52   Math Test: How much money? Grade 3

1. $ 6.16   2. $ 1.46   3. $ 5.56   4. $ 9.00   5. $ 6.36
6. $ 2.95   7. $ 7.06   8. $ 3.80   9. $ 9.30   10. $ 8.05

Page 53   Math Test: What are the coins?

1. 25 25 10 10 10 5   2. 10 1 1   3. 10 10 10 5 5   4. 25 25 1 1   5. $1

Page 54   Math Test: What are the coins?

1. $1 $1 10 10 5 5   2. $1 $1 $1 $1 $1 25 25 10 1 1 1 1   3. $2 25 25 25 5 1 1 1 1
4. $1 $1 $1 $1 25 25 5 1 1   5. $2 $2 $2 $2 25 25 25 10 5 1 1

Page 55   Grade 1 Math Test: Coin Addition

1. 7 ¢   2. 8 ¢   3. 3 ¢   4. 9 ¢   5. 9 ¢

Page 56   Grade 2 Math Test: Coin Subtraction

1. 3 ¢   2. 6 ¢   3. 2 ¢   4. 8 ¢   5. 4 ¢

Page 57   Grade 2 Math Test: Coin Addition

1. 77 ¢   2. 77 ¢   3. 76 ¢   4. 82 ¢   5. 77 ¢

Page 58   Grade 2 Math Test: Coin Subtraction

1.43 ¢   2. 58 ¢   3. 30 ¢   4. 49 ¢   5. 51 ¢

Page 60   Math Test: Telling Time to the Hour #1

1. 7:00   2. 4:00   3. 10:00   4. 5:00
    7 o'clock   4 o'clock   10 o'clock   5 o'clock
5. 8:00   6. 12:00   7. 9:00   8. 3:00
    8 o'clock   12 o'clock   9 o'clock   3 o'clock
9. 6:00   10. 11:00   11. 2:00   12. 1:00
    6 o'clock   11 o'clock   2 o'clock   1 o'clock

Page 61   Math Test: Telling Time to the Hour #2

1. 4:00   2. 8:00   3. 1:00   4. 3:00
    4 o'clock   8 o'clock   1 o'clock   3 o'clock
5. 10:00   6. 6:00   7. 5:00   8. 11:00
    10 o'clock   6 o'clock   5 o'clock   11 o'clock
9. 7:00   10. 12:00   11. 2:00   12. 9:00
    7 o'clock   12 o'clock   2 o'clock   9 o'clock

Page 62   Math Test: Telling Time to the Half Hour #1

1. 8:30   2. 1:30   3. 10:30   4. 5:30
    half past 8   half past 1   half past 10   half past 5
5. 2:30   6. 9:30   7. 11:30   8. 3:30
    half past 2   half past 9   half past 11   half past 3
9. 6:30   10. 8:30   11. 4:30   12. 12:30
    half past 6   half past 8   half past 4   half past 12

Page __63__ Math Test: Telling Time to the Half Hour #2

1. 2:30
   half past 2
2. 6:30
   half past 6
3. 8:30
   half past 8
4. 3:30
   half past 3
5. 1:30
   half past 1
6. 11:30
   half past 11
7. 5:30
   half past 5
8. 9:30
   half past 9
9. 10:30
   half past 10
10. 7:30
    half past 7
11. 12:30
    half past 12
12. 9:30
    half past 9

Page __64__ Math Test: Telling Time to the Quarter Hour #1

1. 2:15
   quarter past 2
2. 4:15
   quarter past 4
3. 1:15
   quarter past 1
4. 5:15
   quarter past 5
5. 8:15
   quarter past 8
6. 6:15
   quarter past 6
7. 3:15
   quarter past 3
8. 11:15
   quarter past 11
9. 9:15
   quarter past 9
10. 12:15
    quarter past 12
11. 7:15
    quarter past 7
12. 10:15
    quarter past 10

Page __65__ Math Test: Telling Time to the Quarter Hour #2

1. 4:15
   quarter past 4
2. 12:15
   quarter past 12
3. 8:15
   quarter past 8
4. 5:15
   quarter past 5
5. 2:15
   quarter past 2
6. 6:15
   quarter past 6
7. 1:15
   quarter past 1
8. 10:15
   quarter past 10
9. 9:15
   quarter past 9
10. 3:15
    quarter past 3
11. 7:15
    quarter past 7
12. 11:15
    quarter past 11

Page __66__ Math Test: Telling Time to the Quarter Hour #3

1. 4:45
   quarter to 5
2. 10:45
   quarter to 11
3. 5:45
   quarter to 6
4. 7:45
   quarter to 8
5. 1:45
   quarter to 2
6. 2:45
   quarter to 3
7. 3:45
   quarter to 4
8. 9:45
   quarter to 10
9. 12:45
   quarter to 1
10. 11:45
    quarter to 12
11. 6:45
    quarter to 7
12. 8:45
    quarter to 9

Page __67__ Math Test: Telling Time to the Quarter Hour #4

1. 6:45
   quarter to 7
2. 11:45
   quarter to 12
3. 5:45
   quarter to 6
4. 9:45
   quarter to 10
5. 3:45
   quarter to 4
6. 12:45
   quarter to 1
7. 7:45
   quarter to 8
8. 10:45
   quarter to 11
9. 1:45
   quarter to 2
10. 3:45
    quarter to 4
11. 4:45
    quarter to 5
12. 8:45
    quarter to 9

Page __68__ Math Test: Telling Time

1. 7:00
2. 1:30
3. 2:00
4. 7:30
5. 10:00
6. 2:30
7. 8:00
8. 6:30
9. 5:00
10. 3:30
11. 9:30
12. 3:00

Page __69__ Math Test: Telling Time

1. 4:45
2. 6:00
3. 8:30
4. 9:15
5. 12:00
6. 5:45
7. 3:30
8. 3:15
9. 11:45
10. 2:15
11. 6;30
12. 10:00

Page _70_ Math Test: Telling Time

1. 9:55	2. 3:50	3. 7:40	4. 5:55
5. 5:25	6. 11:10	7. 6:05	8. 2:10
9. 1:10	10. 4:50	11. 3:35	12. 3:20

Page _71_ Math Test: Elapsed Time

Start Times	End Times	Elapsed Times
1. 10:45	11:10	25 minutes has passed
2. 4:45	12:45	8 hours has passed
3. 6:05	9:30	3 hours and 25 minutes has passed

4. 3:20   What time did Ben return home?
5:30

Page _72_ Math Test: Time

1. B.		2. A.
3. A.		4. A.
5. A.		6. B.
7. B.		8. B.
9. A.		10. A.

Page _73_ Math Test: Days of the Week

1. C.		2. C.
3. A.		4. B.
5. C.		6. B.
7. C.		8. C.
9. B.		10. A.

Page _74_ Math Test: Months of the Year

1. C.		2. B.
3. C.		4. A.
5. B.		6. C.
7. B.		8. A.
9. C.		10. B.

Page _75_ Math Test: Measurement

1. 13 cm   2. 8 cm   3. 10 cm

Pages _76 - 77_ Math Test: Measurement

1. B.   2. A   3. C.   4 . B   5. A   6. C   7. C   8. A

Page _78_ Math Test: Perimeter

A.

1. 16 units   2. 14 units   3. 14 units   4. 18 units   5. B

Page _79_ Math Test: Area

A.
1. 9 units
2. 10 units
3. 10 units
4. 16 units
5. B

Page _82_ Math Test: Patterning and Algebra Grade 2

1. B.	2. A.	3. A.	4. C.	5. A.
6. C.	7. C.	8. B.	9. B.	10. A.

Page _83_ Math Test: Patterning and Algebra Grade 2

11. C.	12. C.	13. A	14. B.	15. A.
16. C.	17. C.	18. A.	19. B.	20. A.

Page _84_ Math Test: Patterning and Algebra Grade 3

1. C.	2. C.	3. C.	4. A.	5. B.
6. A.	7. A.	8. B.	9. B.	10. C.

Page _85_ Math Test: Patterning and Algebra Grade 3

11. A.	12. C.	13. C	14. B.	15. C.
16. A.	17. B.	18. B.	19. B.	20. C.

Page _87_ Math Test: Naming Shapes

1. hexagon
2. pentagon
3. circle
4. square
5. parallelogram
6. rectangle
7. triangle
8. octagon
9. trapezoid
10. rhombus

Page _90_ Math Test: 3D Figures

1. F.
2. E.
3. B.
4. A.
5. D.
6. C.

Page _91_ Math Test: 3D Figures

1. Cylinder
   Faces 2 edges 2 vertices 0
2. Sphere
   Faces 0 edges 0 vertices 0
3. Rectangular Prism
   Faces 6 edges 12 vertices 8
4. Cone
   Faces 1 edges 1 vertices 0
5. Pyramid
   Faces 5 edges 8 vertices 5
6. Cube
   Faces 6 edges 12 vertices 8

Page _92_ Math Test: Geometry Grade 2

1. A.	2. C.	3. B.	4. B.	5. B.
6. B.	7. A.	8. C.	9. B.	10. A.

Page 93 Math Test: Geometry Grade 2

11. B.	12. A.	13. A.	14. C.	15. B
16. A.	17. A.	18. B.	19. C.	20. A.

Page 94 Math Test: Geometry Grade 3

1. A.	2. C.	3. A.	4. C.	5. C.
6. B.	7. C.	8. C.	9. B.	10. B.

Page 95 Math Test: Geometry Grade 3

11. B.	12. A.	13. C.	14. B.	15. A.
16. B.	17. C.	18. B.	19. A.	20. B.

Page 97 Math Test: Reading Pictographs

1. 6   2. 4   3. pears   4. cherries   5. 13

Page 98 Math Test: Reading Pictographs

1. Lemonade	2. Milk	3. 6	4. 10
5. 14	6. 30	7. 8	8. 16

Page 99 Math Test: Reading Tally Charts

1. Blue   2. Green   3. 12   4. 32   5. 6
2. a. blue   b. red   c. purple   d. green

Page 100 Math Test: Reading Bar Graphs

1. Favorite Ice Cream Flavours	2. by 2's	3. Rocky Road
4. Other	5. 10	6. 22 7. 52

Great Job!

_____

Math Expert!

You did it!

_____

Great Work!